FILM

Andrea Gronemeyer studied theater, film and television in Cologne and Florence, and is currently artistic director of the 'Comedia' theater in Cologne.

TAKE YOUR GIRLIE TO THE MOVIES
(IF YOU CAN'T MAKE LOVE AT HOME)

WORDS BY
**EDGAR LESLIE
& BERT KALMAR**

MUSIC BY
**PETE
WENDLING**

FILM

Andrea Gronemeyer

LAURENCE KING

Cover photos from top to bottom and left to right:

Chronophotography by Etienne-Jules Marey, 1882 / Marilyn Monroe in *The Seven Year Itch*, dir. Billy Wilder, 1955 / Charles Chaplin on scene filming *The Gold Rush*, 1924 / Logo of Twentieth Century Fox / Still from *In the Realm of the Senses*, dir. Nagisa Oshima, 1976 / Multiplex movie center in Hannover, Germany / Poster for *Gone with the Wind*, dir. Victor Flemming, 1939 / Alfred Hitchcock with cigar and bird, promotion for his *The Birds*, 1962 / Still from *Metropolis*, dir. Fritz Lang, 1926 / Still from *Fanny and Alexander*, dir. Ingmar Bergman, 1982 / Movie audience in a 3D film in New York / Character from *Toy Story*, dir. John Lasseter, 1995

Back cover photos from top to bottom:

Mickey Mouse and the sorcerer in *Fantasia*, dir. James Algar, 1940 / Steven Spielberg with camera shooting *Jurassic Park*, 1996 / Poster for *The Battleship Potemkin*, dir. Sergei Eisenstein, 1925

Frontispiece:

Musical score for *Take Your Girlie to the Movies (if you can't make love at home)*, popular song, ca. 1919

Many of the illustrations used in this book were taken from the promotion material of different movie and distribution companies whom we would like to thank for their generosity: Columbia Pictures, Lucasfilm Ltd., MGM, Paramount Pictures Corp., RKO-General, United Artists, Universal Pictures, United International Pictures, and Warner Bros.

English text version by: Agents–Producers–Editors, Overath, Germany
Translated by: Paul Dvorak, Richmond, Va.
Edited by: Tammi Reichel, Overath, Germany, and Tina Ennulat, Richmond, Va.

First published in Great Britain in 1999 by Laurence King Publishing
an imprint of Calmann & King Ltd
71 Great Russell Street
London
WC1B 3BN
Tel: + 44 171 831 6351
Fax: + 44 171 831 8356
e-mail: enquiries@calmann-king.co.uk
www.laurence-king.com

Text copyright © 1998 DuMont Buchverlag GmbH und Co.
          Kommanditgesellschaft, Köln, Federal Republic of Germany
English translation copyright © 1998 Barron's Educational Series, Inc., New York

A catalogue record for this book is available from the British Library.

ISBN 1 85669 196 9

Printed in Italy by Editoriale Lloyd

Content

Preface

What is film? The word literally means "skin" and originally designated only the coated celluloid on which the first picture sequences were recorded. The audiences of the earliest "living pictures," shown in 1895, were certainly less enthusiastic about the novel material than about the amazing quality of the reproduction of reality in moving pictures; this popular form of entertainment is still usually referred to in America—and more and more so internationally—as motion pictures or, almost lovingly, the movies.

If one speaks of cinema, however, one uses a term etymologically related to the first machine that successfully took and played back moving pictures, the *Cinématographe* developed by the Lumière brothers. Today cinema generally refers not only to a camera and projector, but to the genre of film as a whole, and sometimes the place where films are shown. In France, where people are justifiably proud of pioneering achievements in the areas of film technique and marketing, there exist not only the ideas of film and cinema, but also *cinématographie*, or film as an artistic genre. To present the technical, economic and aesthetic aspects that manifest themselves in these different ideas is the task of film historians. This concise history, too—almost a history of film in quick-motion—aims to offer not only a chronicle of the masterpieces, but also a history of the technical innovations and economic influences which are decisive for the development of the cinema. Furthermore, as both a means and an object of social communication, film cannot be considered independently of contemporary events, culture and fashion, areas on which it in turn has impact in a variety of ways.

Film is one of the most influential mass media of our time. Around the whole world, at any given time, millions of people are watching films. Movie theaters alone attract about 15 billion spectators annually. Art and experimental films, pure entertainment fare, documentaries, animated cartoons, and, last but not least, advertisements are no longer disseminated solely through the theaters. They reach us via television programs and the Internet, on video and CD-ROM, even on airplanes: Film pursues us. People watch movies to escape from reality or to learn as much as possible about it. Films reflect our dreams and nightmares, the great fears as well as the small romantic longings; film can indoctrinate or clarify, but mostly, in their probably most wonderful function, they "simply" want to entertain us.

This *Concise History of Film* tells not only one, but many histories of film. It cites numbers and facts, but it is neither an encyclopedia of film nor a biographical reference book that claims to be comprehensive. Its goal is to trace lines of development, make connections more understandable, and to direct some spotlights on life both before and behind the camera.

Andrea Gronemeyer

ca. 1000
First description of the *camera obscura* principle by the Arabic scholar Ibn al-Haytham

ca. 1100
Shadow play spreads from China throughout Asia

ca. 1500
The *camera obscura* is introduced to Europe

1590
Invention of the microscope

1608
Invention of the telescope

1671
Earliest description of a magic lantern

1765
James Watt develops the steam engine

1822
Discovery of limelight promotes the spread of the magic lantern

1826
Nièpce successfully makes the first photograph

1830
Opening of the first railroad line between Liverpool and Manchester

1833
Stampfer and Plateau each develop the wheel of life independently of one another

1839
Daguerre introduces the daguerreotype to the public; Talbot exposes images on paper and discovers the process for making negatives

1851
Production of the first sewing machines

Edison's Kinetoscope does not show a movie because a film is shown to a larger public rather than just to an individual viewer.

Who invented the movies?

1895 is considered to be the year that film was born. The race to be the first to present "living photographs" was clearly won by the Skladanowsky brothers in Berlin on November 1, 1895; however, for the history of film the presentation of the Lumière brothers in the Grand Café in Paris eight weeks later on December 28 would receive more credit. Their discovery of the Cinématographe, technically superior to the Skladanowskys' bioscope, is today considered an actual breakthrough for modern film technique. Thomas Alva Edison might also have had a claim to being the originator of the new medium that was changing the world if his Kinetograph, which he submitted for a patent in 1891, and its moving pictures, which aroused amazement in 1893 in a special viewing device, the Kinetoscope, had been accessible to more than one person at a time. But more on that later. The history of the explosive developments of the year 1895 has much earlier roots. Without the "magical" games of the *camera obscura* and the magic lantern there would be no projection; without the discovery of the stroboscopic effect, no illusion of movement; and without photography there would be no images to be set in motion.

The fascination with moving pictures

The picture is the simplest and most generally understood medium for conveying experiences. Since earliest times people have strived not only to represent the world, but to portray it in motion. The precision with which animals, hunters, and dancers are depicted in motion in stone-age cave drawings evokes a sense of wonder. The stories pictured on Egyptian burial friezes are apparently a series of repetitions of the same figures, which upon closer examination reveal themselves to be a very differentiated study of individual phases of movement. These series of reliefs of a running warrior who raises his spear higher and higher,

Max Skladanowsky and his Bioscope.

for example, or of a reaper swinging his sickle, are as close to one another as the successive individual pictures of a filmstrip.

In Asia the concept of projecting moving pictures has been understood for at least a thousand years. The shadow theater so popular in those cultures conjured up gods and heroes, animals from fables, and demons on a screen and portrayed them in various adventures. The earliest remnants of shadow plays were discovered in China and stem from the 11th century. Two-dimensional filigree figures were cut from tanned animal skins and artistically painted in color. The shadow players manipulated the chosen figure's movable limbs with rods right up against the back of a screen of paper or silk. The light from an oil lamp illuminated the figures in such a way that the viewers could even enjoy the moving shadows in color. Especially in Indonesia, the shadow play Wayang Kulit is still popular today, and utilizes black silhouette figures and three-dimensional dolls along with the traditional transparent figures. It is said that modern Indonesian audiences, ever mindful of tradition, still envision encountering the actual spirits of their ancestors in the moving interplay of light and dark.

1874
Introduction of the first electric streetcar in New York
1875
Thomas A. Edison discovers the phonograph, the microphone, and the light bulb
1876
Bell presents his telephone at the World's Fair in Philadephia; Remington produces the first mechanical typewriter
1877
Reynaud presents his Praxinoscope
1882
Marey exposes twelve images in a second on a plate with his "Chronophotograph"
1887
Invention of celluloid roll film
1892
Rudolf Diesel discovers the diesel motor; Edison introduces the Kinetoscope
1894
Opening of a Kinetoscope shop New York
1895
First public films shown by the Skladanowsky brothers in Berlin and the Lumière brothers in Paris

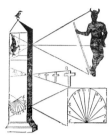

The principle of the *camera obscura* has been known to scientists and scholars since at least the first millennium.

From the *camera obscura* to the camera

Almost all early attempts to project pictures and to set them in motion were prompted by the public's receptivity for purported magic, and were quickly used to feign the effects of supernatural powers. In 16th century Europe sensation seekers allowed themselves to experience fear and terror through the amazing trick box of a traveling Italian by the name of Giovanni Battista della Porta. He invited guests into a darkened room and "magically" produced a devil out of the dark void for the astonished public. Della Porta adapted the principle of the *camera obscura*, first described by the Arab scholar Ibn al-Haitham around the year 1000, to the dark chamber. Al-Haitham had searched for a device that would allow him to observe the eclipse of the sun without injuring his eyes. He discovered that light which enters an otherwise totally dark space through a small opening projects the image of objects and pictures onto the surface in front of the opening for the light. Della Porta placed his public in the *camera obscura* with their backs to the light opening and had an assistant in a devil's costume move around in front of it. The devil appeared to be standing on his head, because the *camera obscura* projects inversely; but it nevertheless had its effect and the new toy quickly spread throughout Europe. Scientists as well as performers adapted the principle for different purposes and accordingly developed it further. It was soon discovered, for example, that a lens mounted into the opening improved the projected picture; by means of a concave mirror or an obliquely placed mirror one could reverse the picture to the "correct" upright position. In the 18th century, a smaller portable *camera obscura* allowed painters and sketchers to reproduce pictures as realistically as possible. They projected the images of objects or landscapes through the hole in the camera onto a piece of sketching paper or a screen and traced them. The desire to capture images directly led to the

The *camera obscura* as an aide for sketching, around 1750.

development of photography in the 19th century, and modern cameras still function according to the optical principle of the *camera obscura.*

First projection with a magic lantern

The prototype of the modern slide projector, the magic lantern, enjoyed great success in Europe at fairs where curiosities and marvelous machines were displayed. A contemporary described them as "a small aide that serves to make ghosts and horrible monsters visible on a white wall and appears to be magic to those who are unfamiliar with the secret." The secret of the magic lantern had already been disclosed by the scholar Anthanasius Kircher in his treatise *Ars magna lucis et umbrae* in 1671. He described a device with which one could project small pictures painted on glass plates onto a white wall. Additionally, a source of light was introduced into a small box, the effect of which was intensified by a concave mirror. The painted glass plates were now inverted between the candle and the single light opening of the box. A convex lens in front of this opening gathered the light shining through the glass picture so that in a darkened room a clear picture could be cast onto the wall.

There is disagreement as to who invented the magic lantern and when it was used for the first time. This sketch by Johannes Zahn originates from 1686.

It was primarily the illiterate populace that was tricked by charlatans and magicians at town fairs. But educated members of fine salons were also duped by business-minded conjurers of ghosts with apparitions of devils, ghosts, and the dead, whose images were dramatically projected into white smoke within the framework of a well-designed performance. Understandably, the secret of the magic lantern itself remained hidden during these spoofs. In the enlightened 19th century, scientists used the practical device to enhance their lectures by projecting explanatory pictures, and the toy industry profitably offered the magic lantern as a sensation for the homes of well-to-do citizens. In the end the discovery of the Cinématographe displaced the magic lantern from the market of curiosities, but without it there would not have been any film premiers in the Grand Café of Paris on December 28, 1895: the Lumière brothers used a magic lantern as the source of light for projecting their films.

Illusion of movement

With the magic lantern an essential prerequisite for cinematography was created: the possibility of projecting pictures before a larger audience. These pictures, however, remained still. The fading in and out of pictures in the magic lantern did not develop into a genuine illusion of movement. Into the 19th century the production of moving pictures continued to depend upon the simultaneous movement of what was being projected. The figures of the shadow theater were moved behind the screen by puppeteers; della Porta's devil had to walk around continuously in front of the aperture of the *camera obscura* in order to be projected in motion on the inside.

However, in order to set photographic images or sketches in motion, a particular optical effect had to be discovered and understood. Perception of the projection of a strip of film as a "living picture," relies upon an optical illusion. A strip of film consists of a series of many distinct pictures, which depict the individual phases of a movement in tiny increments. When the human eye perceives these individual pictures in rapid succession—the optimal rate is twenty-four pictures per second—they blend together into a moving picture. For a long time science had taken the position that this effect was due to the laxity of the human eye, which produces the effect known as persistence of vision. The eye continues to hold the image of a picture for a short time after it has disappeared. Thus the impression of a first image can meld with a second one which follows in quick succession and thus form one picture.

As the magic lantern spread, variations of the device appeared. The use of several lenses, for example, made fade-ins and fade-outs possible. Three-eyed magic lantern around 1885.

The illusion of movement was achieved by mounting two glass pictures over one another and sliding them back and forth in opposite directions during projection. Sliding pictures with two phases of movement from around 1850.

The stroboscopic effect

Today we know that it is only a lightning fast action, the stroboscopic effect, that is responsible for the illusion of movement in film. The rapid sequence of individual pictures only melts into a flow of movement if the projection is interrupted by a short dark phase between the individual pictures. This effect was discovered by the English scientist Michael Faraday, who was attempting to explain why we perceive the movement of a spoked wheel viewed through a lattice fence as stationary or even as moving backwards. He came to the conclusion that an interrupted stream of pictures gives the illusion of a distorted or false picture. The stroboscopic effect not only changes the perception of actual movement, as Faraday determined during his experiments, but under special experimental conditions can also conversely create the illusion of apparent movement.

A wheel brings pictures to life

The Belgian Joseph Plateau and the Austrian Simon Stampfer, independently of one another, used Faraday's discovery to develop a toy that actually produced the first moving picture. Stampfer's Stroboscope and Plateau's Phenakistiscope each consisted of a round disc, on whose outer edge phase pictures of a movement, for example, of a child jumping rope, were painted. In an inner circle below were viewing slits. When viewed in a mirror, the

The thaumatope is a child's toy using the optical effect of persistence of vision. The small piece of paper is painted on the front and back sides. As the bands fastened to the sides are twirled between one's fingers, the piece of paper begins to rotate and the individual pictures blend together into one, like the dancing couple here.

In 1833 toys working on the principle of the wheel of life could be purchased in many countries. The mirror was soon replaced by a second disc on which the phase pictures were painted. When the picture disc was rotated in the opposite direction of the aperture disc, a sharper, clearer picture resulted than in the original design with the mirror.

rotating images as seen through the viewing slits create the impression that the child is actually moving. The dark surfaces between the slits interrupt the view of the little pictures in the mirror, thus producing the stroboscopic effect. This first device for producing a moving picture was given the interesting name "the wheel of life."

More toys

The discovery of the stroboscopic effect aided the discovery and marketing of a series of toys that were equally simple yet amazing. The popular thumb cinema, for example, is nothing more than a tiny book whose pages are printed on one side with a series of phase pictures. When one flips through them quickly between thumb and forefinger, the impression of a moving picture is created. The larger-scale Mutoscope works according to the same principle. In this viewing machine a large number of phase pictures are attached around an axis, which is rotated by a crank or an electric motor. In front of the viewing opening a pin flips the wreath of pictures and entire scenes, such as a boxing match or of a snake dance popular at the time, is presented to the viewer. The magic of the living pictures fascinated the masses and the producers of the new toys accordingly endowed their products with promising names. The Zoetrope, for example, a further discovery that made use of the principle of the wheel of life, was brought to the consumer as the

Mutoscope from 1897.

"wonder drum." The strips of phase pictures mounted on the inner side of such a drum were easily exchangeable so that viewers who looked into the rotating drum through a viewing slit could watch numerous scenes with one and the same viewing device.

Animated screen

An Austrian officer and passionate inventor by the name of Franz von Uchatius came up with the related idea of projecting moving pictures onto a screen in order to make them accessible to a greater public. In 1845 he combined the wheel of life with the principle of the magic lantern. He placed a pane with twelve transparent pictures into the projection machine he had developed. He introduced a lens in front of each picture and rotated the projection light behind the pictures so that they were projected one after the other with the requisite brief dark phase

onto the same point on the screen. This still very cumbersome apparatus became a sales success, although it could only cast movements of very short duration on the wall. Uchatius' plan to build a device with lenses for a hundred pictures was not realized because such a projection device would have been much too complex.

Picture strip to be mounted inside the magic drum.

The first cartoon film

The Frenchman Emile Reynaud was finally successful in projecting cartoon short films onto a screen. In 1877 he had already invented the Praxinoscope. He replaced the viewing slit of the moving drum with a prismatic wreath of mirrors around the rotation axis of the device. The viewer looked at a fixed point on the spinning wreath as the

Praxinoscope.

drum turned in the opposite direction. The multiple mirrors provided the necessary stroboscopic interruption so that a moving picture appeared. In 1888 Reynaud had his "optical theater" patented. With this device he could project layered strips of film into which he had sketched and then colored the phases of movement of small scenes. These transparent filmstrips were already equipped with perforations which allowed the film to be spooled onto another roll. The light of a magic lantern shone through the phase pictures and cast them onto the wreath of mirrors; a second mirror re-directed the illusion of movement onto a screen.

Photographs

In enumerating the discoveries that led to the development of cinematography, the discovery of a French chemist, Joseph Nicéphore Nièpce, cannot be overlooked. The optical process of photography, that of the *camera obscura*, had been understood for hundreds of years before Nièpce, prompted by his fellow countryman, the painter Louis Jacques Mandé Daguerre, discovered a chemical process that would fix the photograph projected into the *camera obscura* directly, without the help of a pencil. Nièpce placed a plate covered with silver nitrate into the camera. It was already known that this solution of extremely fine silver dust turned dark under a beam of light. In 1826 Nièpce was thus able to create the first photograph, but the exposure time was decidedly too long to produce a clear picture. Daguerre then discovered that the image was already latently present after a short exposure time, and became visible if the exposed plate was immersed in a solution of quicksilver in darkness. The picture was then fixed in a salt solution.

Nièpce died before the process was made public (in 1839 before the French Academy of Science), which therefore found wide acceptance and went down in history as the Daguerreotype, without

Poster for Reynaud's
Théâtre Optique.

honoring the deceased partner. Still, daguerreotypes were only inverted, one-of-a-kind pictures which could not be reproduced. More commercially successful was the process of an English competitor who managed to expose an image onto layered paper in the same year as Daguerre's triumph. William Talbot was the first to employ the negative process still used today. Numerous positives, that is, correct images could be copied from his paper photos.

In 1887, the American prelate Reverend Hannibal Goodwin produced the first cellulose nitrate film ribbon. This so-called celluloid had an ultra-thin exposure layer and could be used as roll film in cameras. This discovery propelled the Eastman-Kodak Company, which was independently and almost simultaneously experimenting with celluloid as a material for photos, to emerge as the largest film producer in the world.

Daguerreotype from 1850.

The step toward moving photography

Although photography was invented in 1839 and spread quickly, wheels of life, wonder drums, thumb cinemas, Mutoscopes, Praxinoscopes, and the "optical theater" were only able to transform sketches and paintings into moving pictures. Early photography was not able to capture the smallest intervals of a movement in the successive series of phase pictures necessary to create the illusion of movement. The exposure times were simply too long. The first attempts to meld photographs in a rotating drum into a moving picture were achieved at the expense of considerable torment imposed on the photo models. Thus the dancers that Henry R. Heyl proudly presented in 1870 as the first "living photographs" in his Phantasmatrope—a projection wheel of life with a jerky transport mechanism—had to pose in endless sittings for the exposure time of each individual phase of movement. The resulting flow of movement was, of course, anything but natural. Before the pioneers of cinematography, Edison, the Skladanowskys, and the Lumières, were able to astonish the public with more complex scenic actions and documentary shots, the technical preconditions for instantaneous and sequential photographs first had to be realized.

A bet provides the impetus

The solution was found by researchers who had no interest at all in moving pictures. They were much more intent on using photographic means to capture natural phases of movement, which had not been perceivable by the human eye up to that time. The American Senator Leland Stanford asked himself, for example, in what sequence his horse moved its legs while galloping, and apparently made a bet with a friend that there was actually one moment when all four legs were off the ground at once. In the 1870's he commissioned the renowned English photographer Eadweard J. Muybridge to demonstrate photographically the individual phases of movement. Thanks to the introduction of the instantaneous shutter for lenses, very short exposure times had become possible by then. Muybridge first set up 12, then 24, and finally 100 cameras in shorter and shorter intervals along a race track to take his pictures.

Eadweard Muybridge (1830–1904).

The horse itself caused the pictures to be taken by tripping contact wires that had been drawn across the track as it ran. The principle of series or chrono-photography was invented. Inspired by Muybridge's success, the French physician and movement researcher Etienne-Jules Marey attempted the experiment of sequential photography in 1882 with the development of his "photographic gun." In the barrel of this camera, which was similar to a rifle, he installed a lens with a long focal distance. A timer caused the gun to fire, and the magazine contained up to 25 circular plates containing 12 exposures each. With each rotation of the magazine, 12 individual pictures per second were exposed. The German Ottomar Anschütz, inventor of the slit shutter for extremely short exposure times, came upon the idea of having the photographically fixed movements of animals and people move again. He constructed a viewing machine, the electro-tachyscope, which he made public in 1894. Anschütz mounted exposed series of diapositives on glass plates on a rotating disc behind a viewing hole. The rotating photographs were illuminated individually by a stroboscopic light in front of the viewer and thus restored to their original

Etienne-Jules Marey
(1830–1904).

movement. With the introduction of their clearly superior Cinématographe, the Lumières got a head start on perfecting a planned "rapid view projector."

One of Muybridge's first serial photographs from the year 1878.

From serial picture to moving picture

The universal inventor Thomas A. Edison is one of the most important pioneers in cinematography, even though his film camera, strangely enough, came about only as an afterthought of his research to improve the "phonograph," the precursor of the gramophone. Edison was looking for a way to enhance sound recordings with pictures. Spurred on by Marey's recordings with flexible paper material, he and his assistant William Kennedy Laurie Dickson were the first to experiment with celluloid tape. Edison perforated the strips on both sides with four holes per picture, which made an exact although jerky transport through a toothed wheel mechanism possible, and consequently insured an even interval between pictures. He spooled the rolled up strip through the camera with a crank. Edison set the standards that are still in use today for this perforation and the determination of a tape width of 35 mm.

Edison's "Black Maria" was a black tin hut with a flap roof. The entire studio could be rotated on its own axis so that the sunlight necessary for the photographs could be channeled in different directions. Thomas Alva Edison (1847–1931) was one of the last great universal inventors. He applied for over 1,000 patents for technical discoveries, including the light bulb, phonograph, compound engine, a process for pouring concrete, and the carbon microphone, which made the telephone patented by Bell in 1876 more feasible over greater distances. From 1885 to 1892 he mass-marketed the Kinetoscope, which he rented but did not sell, and could only be used with films of his own production.

In contrast to scientists before him who were primarily interested in precise movement studies, Edison wanted to tell stories with his films from the beginning. He produced film strips of up to thirty seconds in length; previously the series of pictures set in motion could show at most 1–2 seconds. Between 1891 and 1893, Dickson constructed the first film studio in the world for him, the "Black Maria," which owes its name to its similarity to the paddy wagons of the American police at the time. Here, along with numerous variety pieces with dancers, trained animals, and boxers, short skits with titles like *Police Raid a Chinese Opium Den* were made. In 1896 Edison shocked the public with *The Kiss*, a film strip which shows in close-up the first kiss on film. This minute excerpt from the popular stage play *The Widow Jones* provoked what was probably the first film review in history (which reached its climax with the words "totally disgusting"), and nevertheless broke all prior attendance records. As a commercial outlet for his film productions, Edison's research laboratory developed the Kinetoscope, a coin-operated looking box in which an individual viewer could watch a film strip projected onto a matted screen. In 1891 he registered the Kinetograph and the Kinetoscope for patents, but rejected the idea of patenting them for the international market. Edison apparently believed the commercial success of his new toys would be limited, and therefore did not attempt to develop devices for the projection of films before a larger audience. In fact, though, his Kinestoscope shops had already been a sensational success. After the opening of the first "Edison Parlor" in New York on April 14, 1894, the automated halls, also called "Penny Arcades," sprang up like mushrooms in other large American cities as well as in London, Paris, Berlin, and Mexico City.

The actress and actor May Irwin and John C. Rice in the first kiss in film history.

Optical Toys

Camera obscura: Optical principle according to which light entering a dark chamber through a small hole projects a picture from outside inverted and upside down onto the surface opposite the hole.

Laterna magica (magic lantern): oldest projection machine, first operated by candle.

Mutoscope: mechanically driven thumb cinema.

Panorama: Optical show palace, in which visitors are surrounded by a giant, 360° painting around the edge of a round space.

Peepshow or curiosity cabinet: Portable box with viewing holes through which illuminated pictures can be seen on the inside.

Phantasmatrope: Heyl's projection wheel of life with a jerky transport mechanism.

Phenakistiscope: Plateau's wheel of life.

Praxinoscope: The spinning drum further developed by Reynaud in which the viewing slits are replaced with a mirror on the turning axle.

Stroboscope: Stampfer's wheel of life.

Stroboscopic effect: Optical illusion which allows the perception of rapidly shown individual pictures interrupted by a dark phase to melt into a flow of movement.

Thaumatrope: "Magic wheel" which, when turned rapidly, causes two pictures to blend into one due to the effect of persistence of vision.

Thumb cinema: A booklet with phase pictures that is thumbed through.

Wheel of life: A disc whose outer edge is painted with phase pictures and then rotated in front of a mirror. Viewed through the viewing slits of the disc they are perceived as moving pictures

Zoetrope: Spinning "magic drum" for exchangeable phase picture strips which creates the illusion of moving pictures according to the wheel of life principle.

The time is ripe

People's attempts to set pictures in motion and to tell stories by means of moving pictures can be traced back hundreds of years. However, the history of film begins only with the discovery of cinematography, that is, with the technical advances that were made possible primarily by the discoveries of the 19th century. Yet it was not only the tremendous technical progress, but also the fundamental changes in ideas and in society that accompanied the Industrial Revolution, which provided the decisive impetus for further development of the new medium. Industrial mass production with its mechanized processes drew large numbers of people of the same social class with similar desires and needs to the burgeoning metropolitan areas. The separation of work time and leisure time, the transformation of urban life, allowed the new masses to demand diversions and amusements. Their desire for stimulation and hunger for pictures spurred on the development of a market that specialized in products of "mass entertainment." Edison misjudged this trend in the first place with his kinetoscope, which showed a film to individuals hundreds of times instead of presenting a film to hundreds of people at the same time, and secondly by not even patenting this limited invention outside of the United States. Meanwhile, throughout Europe the German theatrical Skladanowsky family, the French

The railroad changed the experience of the environment in the 19th century: space and time were given new value.

photomakers Lumière, and the English photographer Birt Acres and instrument maker Robert William Paul were all at work on projection machines that would make film accessible to a mass audience. The time was ripe for cinematography, and in actuality the technique of film recording and projection was invented

almost simultaneously and independently in these industrialized countries.

Forward-looking actors

The constant search for new attractions for their variety programs led the brothers Max and Emil Skladanowsky to invest free time and money in the development of a device that would simulate "living pictures." They had successfully made their way through Europe with a magic lantern show and had flabbergasted their audiences with apparently moving hazy pictures produced by skillful fade-ins of several projectors. In 1892, the tinkerer Max Skladanowsky made the first German film with a reconstructed Kodak camera on celluloid paper. The photos showed a Berlin street scene and his brother Emil doing gymnastics on the roof of their parents' house. For want of a projector the replay of these films was first seen in thumb cinema form, the small, popular little books one flipped through. Between his performances with the variety show Max worked feverishly on an intermittent mechanism for his projection machine.

Just a flash in the pan: The Bioscope

In May 1895, the double projector, christened the "Bioscope," was finally ready. The directors of the renowned Berlin address for entertainment, the

The panoramas, forerunners of the cinema, were among the offerings for mass entertainment enthusiastically embraced in large cities. In specifically designed circular buildings, 360° paintings presented landscapes or scenes in such a way that the viewers found themselves in the middle of the exhibit.

Around the turn of the century, the theater also made an effort to stage large spectacles and to establish a popular theater movement among the growing masses.

The Bioscope is a double projector which rapidly alternates the projection of two film strips, thus following the model of fading in hazy picture projections. The alternating opening of the two lenses produces the stroboscopic effect and thereby the illusion of movement. For this projection process, the films first had to be cut into individual frames and alternate frames mounted on the two film strips. Since the edited film rolls could only be perforated afterward, the resulting uneven intervals between frames caused severe flutter during replay.

famous "Wintergarten" variety club, personally made the effort to go to the actors' workshop in order to examine the new sensation. Already on November 1, 1895, the short, severely flutter-prone films constituted the climax and conclusion of the program. The public was amazed and the stars of the evening were soon enticed with an invitation from the world-famous variety theater, the Parisian Follies Bergères. The Skladanowskys were acclaimed as the first to publicly show films. But the technology of the Bioscope was too cumbersome to fully establish itself. When the Skladanowkys arrived in Paris on December 29, the whole city was already talking about the Cinématographe of the Lumière brothers, who had shown their "living pictures" to the public just the day before. The Follies Bergères abruptly canceled the already outmoded Bioscope performances. As curious as they were disappointed, the Skladanowskys immediately attended the next performance of their competitors and recognized the technical superiority of the Parisian discovery.

The first film recordings of the Skladanowsky brothers showed short variety skits: a serpentine dance, a humorous act on the horizontal bar, and a boxing kangaroo.

The Skladanowskys' Bioscope is only one of many projection machines that were patented around 1895 in France, England, Germany, the United States, and Italy. The earliest public film presentations also took place simultaneously in all these countries. But the only machines that survived were those whose inventors had the financial backing necessary to further develop and successfully market them.

Entrepreneurs run the race

At the time cinematography was born, research interest and entrepreneurial spirit joined hand in hand. The brothers Auguste and Louis Lumière were just as much passionate inventors as they were enterprising photo producers. When the owner of a Parisian Kineoscope shop approached them in 1894 with the request to develop a filming system which would produce moving pictures more cheaply and could be marketed more profitably than the expensive Edison imports, they immediately set to work.

Auguste and Louis Lumière.

Apparently during one single productive night—after a half-year of preliminary work—Louis Lumière invented the Cinématographe, a compact apparatus that served as recording, copying, and playback machine in one. He took over Edison's film format and perforation, but the revolutionary innovation of his machine was the installation of a shuttle and claw mechanism inside the camera which moved the film past the recording lens in a jerky motion. In the Cinématographe, the film stopped for a split second in front of the lens, an individual picture was exposed, the shutter closed and the claw moved the film along, taking sixteen pictures per second in this way. The intermediary transport mechanism and the rapid opening and closing of the lens produce the necessary stroboscopic effect when playing back the films through the Cinématographe; the Lumières used a magic lantern as the light source which projected the film onto the screen through the open Cinématographe from

The compact Cinématographe of the Lumière brothers could take pictures, make positive copies, and with an additional light source, even project films.

behind. For the production of a positive film, the negative was first placed exactly over an unexposed film strip in the Cinèmatograph and copied by being exposed again.

A Maltese cross to combat flutter

From today's vantage point the early projection machines made by the Lumières and other film

"Forgotten Pioneers"

Louis Aimé Augustin Le Prince (1842–1890) constructed a single-lens camera-projector back in 1888; it was equipped with a Maltese cross gear that transported perforated celluloid film. In 1890 he boarded a train for a demonstration and disappeared without a trace before he could apply for patents for his discoveries. A victim of the cut-throat competition among the pioneers of film?

In 1889 the English photographer William Friese-Greene (1855–1921), along with his partner Mortimer Evans, applied for a patent for a camera and was among the first to utilize celluloid film. A subsequent patent from 1894 also contains the description of a projection machine.

The photographer Birt Acres (1854–1918) received a patent in May 1895 for a camera and developed a projector which he used to give his first public showing in January 1896; however, he was not interested in any commercial exploitation of his discovery. His first films, among them the famous filmstrip "Rough Sea at Dover" were made for the instrument maker Robert William Paul (1869–1943), who had played an essential part in the development of the camera. After Paul and Acres parted ways, Paul improved the camera and introduced his own projector, the "Theatrograph," in February 1896. In contrast to other pioneers, Paul sold his machines and in so doing decisively spurred on the development of the film industry in England and also abroad.

Between 1892 and 1894 Georges Demeny (1850–1917) developed in several stages a recording and projection machine, which, had it been exploited more opportunely, would have anticipated the success of the similarly constructed Cinématographe. It was not until 1896 that the Parisian producer Léon Gaumont introduced it to the marketplace under the name Chronotograph.

In 1894 the American C. Francis Jenkins patented a camera under the name of Phantascope. Together with his countryman Thomas Armat, he presented a projector in October 1895, which he turned over to Edison to be marketed under the name "Edison's Vitascope" after several improvements were made. The Vitascope helped spread movies throughout the United States and Edison firmly established himself as the inventor of the "moving pictures."

oneers delivered very unsatisfactory pictures. The
m strips, which ran out of the projectors onto the
oor, were damaged during each showing and often
re.

The pictures fluttered severely and the motion
ppeared unnatural because the crank speed of the
meraman was of course different from that of the
rojectionist.

One of the most important pioneering
evelopments of the early years was therefore the
ddition of a Maltese cross into the transport
echanisms of almost all commercial projectors
ter 1896. It was the Maltese cross that first made
ossible a smooth transport of the film in regulated
ncrements, thus establishing the preconditions for
utter-free projection.

By 1897 the discovery of cinematography was for
e most part complete. Film technique advanced
ontinuously and was nearly perfected in about 100
ears. Today 24 pictures per second are taken as
pposed to 16 to 20. It was discovered that this
ecording speed produces the most complete illusion
f movement. The projection was improved in the
ollowing way by intensification of the stroboscopic
ffect: each individual picture is additionally
nterrupted one or two times by the lens, so that the
iewer receives not only 24, but 48 or 72 picture
mages per second. The discovery of sound film
1927), the spread of color film (since 1936), the
xperiments with wide screen and three-dimensional
novies, the development of cartoon techniques, and
ast but not least, the use of computer animation in
he place of real-life recording will be addressed in
hapters to follow.

he first films for movie theaters: ocuments of everyday life

ack to the beginnings: The Lumières had already
resented their discovery to an audience of
pecialists in March 1895; on December 28 the first

The introduction of the Maltese cross is credited to Oskar Messter (1866–1943). Before him the Sklada-nowskys, Le Prince, R. W. Paul and others had actually experiment-ed with this device, but the Berlin inventor, director, and founder of the German film industry was instrumental in its breakthrough.

The Maltese cross gear transports and stops the film with optimal timing. As the film starts to turn, the pin is inserted into the slit of the cross, which is connected to the transport roller. When the pin exits from the slit again, the stop plate holds the cross and prevents the film from slipping.

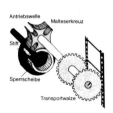

The first films to be shown publicly contain one scene filmed with a stationary camera: *Feeding Baby*.

public performance finally took place in the cellar room of the Grand Café in Paris. The 25 minute program consisted of ten documentary short films. The Lumières began their film production like today's typical home video makers and captured first very normal everyday scenes of their surroundings on celluloid: workers leaving the Lumière factory, Mr. and Mrs. Lumière feeding their baby, men drinking beer and playing cards. The public was surprised by how much the moving pictures looked like real life. Being able to distinguish beer foaming and cigarette smoke moving through the air caused a great stir. *The Arrival of a Train at the Station in La Ciotat* terrified the audience, according to some of the earliest film reviews, because the train appeared to be traveling directly at them. One has to remember, however, that this anecdote arose within the framework of an advertising campaign for the cinema, in order to emphasize the illusion of reality created by the new medium. Among the very earliest of the Lumières' filmstrips was also a short drama. *The Waterer gets Watered* tells the story of a gardener who wonders why no water is coming out of his garden hose. He looks into it and a stream of water promptly sprays him in the face. The public laughed along with the

Instinctively the Lumières grasped what most fascinated their public: rediscovering themselves and their contemporaries in real movement on a screen. *Workers Leaving the Lumière Factory*.

little boy who had been standing on the hose, and then had to run away from the angry gardener.

The Cinématographe conquers the world

Of the 100 seats offered in the basement of the Grand Café for an entrance fee of one franc, only 35 were occupied the first evening, presumably mostly by friends and coworkers of the producers. Enthusiastic newspaper reviews cranked up ticket sales, and soon people were lining up in front of the cinemas that were sprouting up everywhere. A wonderful new business took shape! At first the Lumières did not sell their machines, but kept their inner workings top secret and licensed them to carefully selected lessees. They trained professional cameramen, so-called operators, in cinematography and sent them off on exhausting trips all over the world. It was their job to introduce the technical innovation wherever possible, entice potential purchasers, and simultaneously begin filming other countries, peoples, and customs, because the demand for new filmstrips was growing relentlessly.

Thus the history of film began in many places with the arrival of the Lumières' Cinématographe, which was technically superior to all other devices and was marketed in the quickest, most professional manner. In 1896 there were showings in Brussels, Madrid, St. Petersburg, Cologne, Bombay, Sidney, Shanghai, Mexico City, and Alexandria. By 1897 the demand for cameras and projectors was so great throughout the entire world that the Lumières could no longer meet it with their small company and their patent for manufacturing the machine was sold to the entrepreneur Charles Pathé. The Parisian photo producers considered the success of the cinema a passing phenomenon. They thought the new technology would at best find useful adaptation in the future for

The first movie poster shows the Lumière Cinema as an attraction for the whole family.

While the first order of business was to capture movement, the cameramen themselves were soon set into motion. They filmed from moving boats and trains—the mobile camera was discovered.

The thrill of moving pictures from everyday life soon lost its luster. People who had never left their home town now wanted to see what the world looked like thousands of miles away from them. *Coolies in the Streets of Saigon.*

research. Pathé, on the other hand, recognized the signs of the times and within a few years built up the world's first film empire as a producer of cameras, projectors, and films. The discovery of the film established one of the most profitable economic sectors of the rapidly approaching 20th century.

A magician of the screen

Among the first visitors to the performances in the Grand Café was the actor Georges Méliès. Fascinated by the possibilities of the technical marvel, he spontaneously offered the Lumières 10,000 francs for their discovery, because from this point on the presentation of films was to form the main attraction of his variety program. When the photo producers declined, because they thought only of their own commercial exploitation of the Cinématographe, the enterprising theater director and imaginative inventor of his own magic tricks did not give up. By 1896, he had succeeded in constructing his own camera after he had acquired one of the Englishman R.W. Paul's projectors and studied it carefully.

While the Lumières were exclusively interested in photographing movement and replicating reality, the illusionist Méliès used the new technology to manipulate and alienate the reality represented. He staged fairy tales, fairies, comedies and continual magic tricks for the cinematic showings on his variety stage, which he soon converted entirely to a film theater. When the shutter of his camera jammed, he discovered the possibility of taking trick pictures. In filming the fairy tale *Cinderella* (*Cendrillon*, 1899), for example, he kept the camera running, replaced the pumpkin in the stage picture with a carriage, and the magic in the final film was perfect. Beyond the magical effects of these stop tricks and double exposures, however, Méliès

Georges Méliès (1861–1938) was producer, cameraman, author, and director of his films, and usually appeared as the main actor, as well in projects like *The Man with the Rubber Head* from 1902. In 1907 he wrote about the cinematic tricks he had discovered and the future of the new medium: "Since I have used all kinds ..., I have no hesitation in stating that film today is capable of realizing the most improbable and extraordinary things."

developed no other particular cinematic methods. He remained tied to a rather conventional aesthetics for the theater and filmed his two-dimensional diorama stage with cardboard props from one stationary position.

In 1896, Méliès erected the first European film studio, a 50 foot long (17 m) glass structure. Of the 500 films he produced here, only about 100 have been preserved. Méliès' films enjoyed enormous popularity and were imitated all over the world. His film adaptation of Jules Verne's *A Trip to the Moon* and the "reconstructed reality" of *The Dreyfus Affair* became famous, the latter already a half-hour long documentary. But the craftsman Méliès was quickly overrun by rapidly increasing competition from industrial production. He lost his entire fortune in a series of bad investments and, like the Lumière Brothers before him, left the field of film-making to the master marketer Pathé. In 1938, after having survived for years as a toy dealer, the pioneer of film entertainment died in an old-age home for "cinematographers."

Méliès was the first film director to stage 16 minute-long action films with many different settings and have them colored by hand. *Paris-Monte Carlo in Two Hours* (1905).

Early Film Technique

Bioscope: Projection machine of the Skladanowsky brothers, a double projector with two projection lenses

Black Maria: Name of the first film studio, built by Edison

Celluloid: Oldest thermoplastic man-made material of cellulose, from which the Eastman-Kodak Company has produced flexible film recording tapes (roll film) since 1887

Cinématographe: combined recording, copying, and projecting machine of the Lumière brothers

Electrotachyscope: viewing device developed by Anschütz for showing "living photographs"

Kinetograph: Edison's first film camera

Kinetoscope: Viewing device for Edison's first films

Maltese cross gearing: Intermittent transport mechanism that functions uniformly, allowing a flutter-free picture to be projected

"Théâtre Optique": Reynaud's projection device for showing cartoons along the principle of the Praxinoscope

Vitascope: Projection machine developed by Thomas Armat and distributed by Edison

An explosive beginning

No period in the history of film and cinema was subject to such change as the period of growth known as the Childhood Years, which lasted until the outbreak of the First World War. Developments followed one after the other: Only fifteen years passed between the first fluttering projections of one- to two-minute "living pictures" and the showing of evening-length feature films in classic Hollywood cinema style. The technical sensation of variety shows and county fairs advanced to become an independent art form. By 1908, film was already a mass medium in Europe and America, drawing millions into the movie palaces offering what had become people's primary leisure entertainment. A new branch of the economy had been born, one that brought in enormous profits.

Cinematography, which was invented because scientists and technicians wanted to document movement, discovered its fundamental building block in the movement and dynamics of the chase. It then freed itself from the pure filming of everyday life, as well as from the aesthetics of the theater, and began to develop the specific visual technique for the art of filmmaking.

From traveling cinema to movie theaters

The first showings of the cinematographs, Theatrographs, Bioscopes, and Vitascopes took place in the back rooms of cafés and pubs, or as one element among many in variety programs, vaudeville theaters, and music halls. But the attraction of the

The silent film was never silent. Again and again, there were attempts to present "moving pictures" joined with a mechanical sound device. Even more popular was the incidental music with piano, harmonium, or even a full orchestra in better establishments.

CHRONOMÉGAPHONE L.GA

spectacular technical innovation quickly subsided and, when the interest of the educated citizenry waned, the cinema found a new, enthusiastic public at the fairs of Europe and America. Itinerant performers carried projectors and collections of short films they had purchased throughout the country. The early programs offered a colorful mixture of "living pictures" from all over the world, including actual or re-enacted recordings of battle scenes and state visits, short sketches, and filmings of acrobatic acts and magic tricks. Average white- and blue-collar workers formed the audience for this simple, economical form of entertainment, which was often shown only on an improvised screen of bed linens in a tent with folding chairs. The immigrants in New York loved the cinema above all, because they could enjoy the magic of pictures without having to master a foreign tongue and were introduced to customs and habits of the new world.

The first full-length films were commented on during the performance by film commentators. From 1905 on, comments were copied sporadically onto film strips. They only became commonplace years later, since the un-educated and largely illiterate audiences of the early years con-sidered them an interruption of the film.

In light of the constantly growing demand for entertaining films, the establishment of permanent movie theaters proved to be an ingenious marketing idea. In the United States, cinema owners offered series of "one reelers," short, 10 to 15 minute one-act films whose 600 to 1000 feet of film just fit onto one reel, for a price of only 5 cents in their so-called Nickelodeons. The one- to two-hour programs of the Nickelodeons typically offered a colorful potpourri from various genres.

The so-called chase film was especially popular, where, in each case, a different pursuit made up the central plot. People could not get enough of this wild spectacle, which showed a policeman chasing after a criminal, a woman on her husband's heels, or an angry crowd after a man with no pants on. In the

The Harris brothers created the prototype of the Nickelodeon in Pittsburgh. This new movie theater was open six days a week, from eight in the morning until midnight, and changed the program and the audience every 15 minutes so that 7000 to 8000 people could attend the performances daily.

When the first evening-length feature films came to the market, the modest Nickelodeons and cinema shops were gradually replaced by lavishly decorated movie palaces with over 1000 seats. The expanding business made it possible to include other groups of patrons who could afford the cost. Movie palace in Seattle, 1926.

chase film, the filmmakers began to explore movement between two spatially separate venues, freeing the camera from its stationary position as a member of a theater audience. In the chase, they discovered the most elemental means of creating cinematic tension, which occurred not only in scenes on foot but also on horseback, on trains, and in automobiles, constantly increasing the tempo. Today the chase is still part of the standard repertoire of the criminal film, the western, the thriller, and the action film.

From film craft to film industry

Throughout the entire United States, Nickelodeons were springing up like mushrooms; five years later there were already 10,000 permanent movie theaters in the country, considerably more than in all the European countries combined. America represented the largest sales market for the popular new attraction and provided considerable profits to national and international film producers. Because of low production costs, the export possibilities for film-makers in these early years were so good that innovative producers in small countries, such as the Danish firm Nordisk or the Italian Cines, were able to compete on the international market. The Organization of Film Producers had to be fully reorganized and restructured between 1905 and 1910.

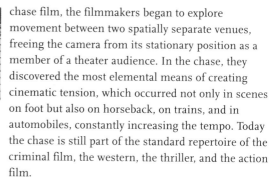

The pioneers of cinematography, Lumière, Méliès, and Paul, continued to produce their films as craftsmen. They built their equipment in their own workshops, acted, directed, stood behind the camera, distributed their own copies and finally worked the projectors in their own theaters. In the long run, this ineffecient production and distribution system did not allow them to meet the growing demand for equipment and for new, more complex film narratives. Entrepreneurs who were willing to take the risk filled the gap and built up an increasingly job-specific, capital-based film industry with the aid of powerful financial backers. Ultimately, the sale of copies no longer made sense. The final death blow to the itinerant cinematograph came with the world-wide introduction, in 1907, of the more profitable rentals system.

The French concern Pathé Frères dominated the world market until the outbreak of the First World War, which would severely damage the European film economy and cause it to lag further behind the expanding American competition from that point on. Before 1914, Pathé himself had distributed twice as many films as all the American providers combined; by 1913 the concern, which had begun production in 1896 with a start-up capital of 24,000 Francs, had a value of 30 million Francs. Caricature poster from the year 1908.

The call for cinematic art

Around 1907, international film production suffered its first crisis. The monotony of film offerings began to bore the public; the stream of viewers stagnated. The educated public began to reject the predominantly simple, slap-stick, or frivolous little films of the early years. In Germany, the stronghold of theatrical culture, a heated debate flared about the value, or lack thereof, of the new mass entertainment media. A cinema reform movement called for a "general education campaign against filth and scandal." For conservative representatives of the bourgeois intelligentsia, the cinema was "mindless, unimaginative fare," which helped "triviality gain victory and corrupt the

The success of the famous film d'art, *The Assassination of the Duke de Guise* of 1908, seemed well-planned and inevitable. The main roles were played by the well-known actors of the *Comédie Française*, and the symphonic music accompanying it on a gramophone record originated from no less than the pen of Camille Saint-Saëns.

Considerably more successful than the film d´art was the serial film, which was also conceived in France. In a series such as, for example, Louis Feuillade's five-part film about the mysterious criminal *Fantômas*, the narrative traced the plot line through a series of short sequences, each ending with a climax, or "cliff-hanger," in order to lure the audience back to the next installment. Thus the serial film created a type of transition from the one-reeler to the feature film in the first decade of the century.

taste of the populace." Film producers who wanted to spread their wares to a new sector of the public therefore tried to raise standards by engaging well-known authors and stage actors, and by building representative premiere performance cinemas in the style of the ornate temples of the theater.

In France in 1907, the Lafitte brothers founded a society to produce so-called art films, the "Compagnie des Films d'art." Its program of ambitious films of literary works was received immediately by the critics and the middle-class public as an improvement over the poor quality of the popular entertainment. But the film d'art only mimicked the theater. The actors moved with gestures and mime-like techniques that looked ridiculous on the screen.

The stationary camera captured stilted pictures of directing techniques, dramatic effects, and stage settings governed by theatrical conventions. Such poor replicas aroused, at best, as one skeptical reviewer wrote, the longing for genuine theater. The reversion to the dramatic play led into an artistic dead-end and failed, as well, to achieve the desired economic success for the producers.

The Brighton School

Just after the turn of the century, there arose a group of filmmakers from Brighton, who delved into the specific components of cinematic language in order to make their plots more comprehensible, exciting, and entertaining. The portrait photographer George Albert Smith (1864–1959) was the first to experiment with technical narrative possibilities, which come about when a scene is composed of various individual shots and camera perspectives. In his film *The Mouse in the Art School* we see, for example, a group of female art students drawing, who suddenly begin to scream and jump up on tables and chairs. The cause of the excitement, a mouse looking out of its hole, Smith shows between the two groups of girls in a close-up. Smith had found a way to explain cinematographically an occurrence which had only been possible to convey on the theatrical stage by the use of language. Thus he had recognized that film can establish meaning through the relationship of pictures to one another.

The former pharmacist James Williamson (1855–1933) had already discovered in 1899 that cinematic narrative did not necessarily have to show the entire duration of an action in order to be understood. In the the actual filming of a rowing regatta, Williamson inserted a shot between the start and finish of the race and was the first to use the central device of the selective elliptical montage. In *Attack on a Mission in China*, he went a step farther and cross cut pictures of a missionary woman screaming for help, having fled from her attackers to a balcony, and the rescuers rushing to save her. Today, this film technique of the "last-minute rescue" still forms the inevitable dramatic highpoint of many westerns, thrillers, and action films.

The English filmmakers from Brighton, who were the first to use cinematic means of expression, had no opportunity to develop their innovations further. The relatively unsupported Brighton "craftsmen" could not keep pace with growing competition from the international film industry.

"Craftsmen" film production in Brighton: developing film, making copies, quality control.

G. A. Smith's film *Grandmother's Reading Glass* is an example of the early use of the insert cut, the direct exchange of extremely different shot sizes, and of the point-of-view shot, which recreates the subjective perspective of a character. Smith continuously cuts the picture through the eyes of the child looking through the reading glass against the close-ups of the observed objects, such as the eye of the grandmother (circular excerpt in front of black background).

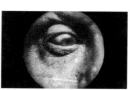

J. Williamson also knew the effect of the close-up. In *The Big Swallow* a man who does not want to be photographed moves annoyedly toward a firmly planted camera until we see only his wide-open mouth on the screen. After editing, the interior of his mouth is replaced with a black background, and we are forced to experience how the filmer disappears together with his camera inside it. A further cut returns back to the open mouth, the man laughs and chews triumphantly.

Enrico Guazzoni's *Quo vadis?* becomes a box-office success in 1913 in Berlin, Paris, and New York. The public was enthralled by the skillful shot changes and the bloody persecution of the Christians with real lions and 5000 extras in the scene.

Monumental spectacles from Italy

Independent film production began in Italy only around 1905. The cinema, however, did not have to travel through towns as a cheap county-fair attraction. From the beginning, it drew a viewing audience from all levels of society to permanent movie theaters. It was therefore no wonder that the Italians were rather more inclined to accept and utilize the cinema as a more artistic medium. Their formula for development of cinematic art was, however, not directed towards the theater. Instead, the Italians brought the narrative and visual potentials of film to light. They demonstrated that film could conquer time and space and could create larger relationships, as an epic rather than dramatic medium.

The newly established film companies Cines, Itala, and Ambrosio specialized in elaborate filmings of historical events, mostly based on popular literary formulas. With a large amount of investment capital, they expanded the cinematic space that could be portrayed by filming outdoors with gigantic sets constructed of "hard" materials

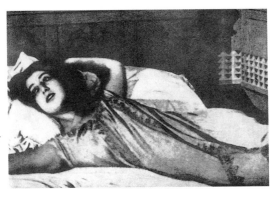

Among the first divas of the Italian cinema, where the cult of acting goddesses began earlier than in other countries were Lyda Borelli (right) and the theatrical star Eleonora Duse.

and at the original sites of national history. Pompei's ready-made army of extras populated the scenery and awed the international public. After the world-wide success of the twenty-minute historical drama *The Last Days of Pompei*, the producers set their sights on longer and more complex cinematographic epics. Films with titles like *The Fall of Troy* (30 min., 800 extras), *Agrippina* (50 min., 2000 extras), and *Quo vadis?* (120 min., 5000 extras) were large-scale investment risks that were supposed to pay off quickly. Italy rose within less than two years to become, along with France, the country with the highest export share of films.

For the film *Cabiria*, the largest international film production project of its time, the Italian prince of poetry Gabriele D'Annunzio was hired as the author. However, in the end he only wrote several commentary inserts and charged a considerable sum for the use of his name.

In 1914, with a million gold Lira, the Itala produced the most costly film of those early years, with the longest showing time of three hours and fifteen minutes: *Cabiria*. With the help of masses of people, elephants, camel caravans, and fantastic stage sets, the director Giovanni Pastrone spared no effort in setting the scene, with its richness of historical plot elements, between high-mountain snow and desert. *Cabiria* is also an example of the cinematographic richness that Italian monumental film had achieved at its highest point. Pastrone worked with different shot sizes, varied shot lengths and cutting and editing sequences, experimented with alternating montage, and was one of the first to employ artificial light for aesthetic purposes. For the outdoor shots he constructed a camera car and established the possibilities of the moving camera as a new cinematic means of expression. The "carello," which Pastrone even had patented after the completion of the film, opened up a new dimension for cinematography: the depth of space.

The seductive "Danish Kiss," during which the lips are joined for a long time and the woman inclines her head back in ecstasy, charmed the public and set precedents.

Denmark: Cinematic dramatic art

In the early years of the cinema, producers from small countries were also able to establish themselves in the international market—assuming they understood business practices and had a nose for sensationalism. The Danish Nordisk Films Compagni was founded in 1906 by the former circus acrobat Ole Olsen. In 1907, for his safari-film *Lion Hunt*, he had two large, live lions killed in front of a moving camera. The vociferous protests promoted sales; Olsen sold a world-wide total of 260 copies of the film strip. In 1910, he created an international furor with his first full-length film, *The White Slave*. The story of a European woman who is dragged off to a bordello in a foreign land unleashed, again, a public outcry as well as a call for film censorship because of its "dangerous sensuality." It was one of the first in a series of erotic films for which the Scandinavian producers of the pre-war years were to become famous.

Asta Nielsen (1881–1972) was one of the first great film stars. Following the international success of her Danish films, Berlin producers brought her to Germany, where she was one of the most beloved actresses up until the time of the sound film.

The Danish pioneers earned themselves special recognition in promoting techniques of cinematic acting. The theatrical star Asta Nielsen had recognized "that the all-revealing lens ... promotes the highest reality of expression," and that cinematic acting demanded a totally different form of representation than the theater. Under the direction of her husband Urban Gad, in her first film *Abysses* in 1910, Asta Nielson demonstrated the myriad new possibilities of cinematic acting in how, with tiny gestures, a glance, a movement of the head, and with the sensual presence of her entire body, she was able to

reveal a full range of emotions. The "Queen of the Silent Film" was the preferred actress in roles portraying the tragic lover or the persecuted innocent, whose fate inevitably took a tragic turn. The Danes, who had made the unmasking of the soul popular on the screen, ruled the German film market until the end of the First World War and founded the Scandinavian tradition of the psychological film with their melodramas.

The films of Nordisk owed their world-wide success to extraordinary stylistic means including an artistic use of light, melodramatic material, realistic props, and the intensity of their natural and reserved actors.

From New York to Hollywood:
The Americans conquer the world market

The early years of American film production were marked by a flood of legal suits. Until 1905, wrestling over patents restricted development; a second ten-year round of legal wrangling was carried out between a film cartel introduced by Edison (MPPC) and independent producers. But attempts at monopolization failed. The independents, who almost all came from the cinema profession, knew the tastes of their public better, and in adapting to the long "feature" film and introducing the star system, introduced the more successful concept. They produced the first slapstick comedies and film epics with great success, while Edison's cartel could lay claim to the discovery of the western. Hollywood, where the independents then moved their production sites in order to avoid control by the MPPC, established itself as the new production center. The good weather and the many different types of landscapes in California offered optimal conditions for filming. By 1914, 50 percent of all films distributed world-wide were already being produced in Hollywood.

The first American film star, Florence Lawrence (1888–1938), was only known to her fans as the "Biograph Girl." The early film producers never named their actors at the end of the film, because they wanted to hinder the development of a star cult in order to keep salaries low. It was the independent producers who first introduced the star system and began to use actors' names for marketing purposes.

The first showdown

Edwin S. Porter did not exactly invent the western, but he did direct the genre's first great cinematic success in 1903, with *The Great Train Robbery*. Films with western motifs had already been seen in Edison's Kinetoscope shops. The western has

The western exaggerated the bloody reality of the settling of the American west in pictures about freedom and manliness in the "Land of Unlimited Possibilities." The last shot from *The Great Train Robbery*, one of the first westerns in the history of film.

been one of the most stable types of film throughout cinematic history; however, its popularity had been limited—with some exceptions—to the United States. Similar to the Italian monumental film, which, with its rendering of a revered past, mirrored the awakening national consciousness of a recently unified Italy, the western fulfilled people's need for national myths. The film was no longer just sensationalistic and nerve-wracking; it had become a medium with a social message. With *The Great Train Robbery*, a story composed of several scenes, Porter popularized fundamental narrative components in the picture film, and the use of these were soon imitated in international films. Racing scene changes and pan shots within scenes produced tension and manipulated the dynamics of tempo in the film.

Rescued by Rover (1905), a film by the British director Cecil M. Hepworth (1874–1953). About the rescuing of a kidnapped baby is told according to the same principles as Porter's *The Great Train Robbery* and shows how quickly aesthetic advances during the first decade of the history of film were adapted.

Next, Porter narrated two plot lines independently of one another—still without placing them parallel—eventually bringing the two parties involved, the criminal bandits and their pursuers, to the final test of strength. This so-called showdown, even today the classical climax of the western genre, reached its climax in *The Great Train Robbery* in a close-up that was sensational for the early cinema: the leader of the robbers draws his pistol and aims it at the audience.

The art and rules of editing

The most important director of early American film production, and a groundbreaker in the classical Hollywood cinema, was David W. Griffith. From 1908 until 1913, he produced almost 450 one-reelers for the Biograph. He had a falling-out with his financial backers when he filmed his first full-length film, the historical drama *Judith of Bethulia*, against the express opposition of the company.

David W. Griffith (1875–1948) with his favorite cameraman Billy Bitzer (1874–1944). Griffith came to the movies as an actor and gained fame through the further development of montage technique. Bitzer demonstrated extraordinary virtuosity in handling the camera; in his late films the especially sentimental lighting technique is striking.

Disappointed by the low level of risk tolerance by the trustees of the Biograph, Griffith fled to the independent producers, for whom he was able to realize his most historically important cinematic projects. He is generally recognized as the inventor of film montage, because he had joined together the most important innovations of European cinema and developed them further. Like the filmmakers from Brighton, whose films were very popular in America, he experimented with the insert cut. He recognized that an individual shot, rather than the scene, comprises the central element of cinematic language, and expanded the repertoire of new, varied shot sizes. He not only used the full scope of long shots, medium shots, close-ups, and extreme close-ups, he also combined them in increasingly free, rapid, and action-filled sequences.

The Birth of a Nation was one of the first so-called "blockbusters," a monumental film in which an enormous amount was invested. It cost 110,000 dollars …

... *Intolerance* the rather reckless sum of 1.9 million dollars.

The many cuts increased the complexity of the films. In order to avoid false connections, Griffith therefore had to make sure that temporal and spatial logic was preserved. He developed the guidelines for continuity editing, which, from that point on, would guide the realistic narrative film of the classical Hollywood cinema. According to this system, every scene must be introduced by an establishing shot, an opening scenic long shot. To avoid jarring movement of the picture, the shot following the cut should use a new camera angle and picture excerpt. So that positioning and posture of the characters, and other important picture elements, blend in the appropriate shots, they must be tediously checked after each cut; the plot line established between two people may not, for example, jump ahead during the change of camera position. Griffith developed a preference for the cross cutting, or intercutting, of Williamson and utilized it with great skill to heighten tension.

Encouraged by the international success of Pastrone's *Cabiria*, he took a chance with his first monumental film epic *The Birth of a Nation* in 1915. The two-and-a-half hour film depicts the history of the American Civil War through the points-of-view of typical families from the North and the South, who, having been friends before the War, have to fight in it against one another. The film unleashed a heated public discussion because of its racist propaganda against the abolition of slavery. In order to defend himself against the charge of being a racist, Griffith undertook a still more ambitious project in 1916 with *Intolerance*.

This three-and-a-half-hour monumental film was comprised of four complete stories illustrating the eternal problem of human intolerance through

Scene from *Birth of a Nation* with Lillian Gish (1893–1993), who as the symbol of injured innocence became a star not only in Griffith's films.

examples of different cultures and eras. With the help of parallel editing, Griffith ran all of the episodes simultaneously, which, in its final sequence, presented the problem of bringing several "last-minute rescues," using relatively small parallel montages, together with a large alternating editing sequence. The innovative director was the first to use a crane, from which the cameraman Billy Bitzer could film the Babylonian palace from a bird's-eye view, in sweeping pan shots.

Cross cutting or intercutting: Rapid change between shots of two simultaneous plots separated by space.

Cut-in: A shot is cut into a scene without disturbing the continuity, mostly as an extreme close-up.

Elliptical editing: Editing form which edits out unimportant segments of an action and reduces them to the most important stages of the development.

Feature film: Narrative film usually based on a filmscript and distinct from other types of film, such as documentary films, experimental films, film essays and animated film.

Genre: A group of films that share a series of similar thematic and stylistic characteristics and consistently proceed according to similar patterns, such as the western, the horror film, the melodrama, and the gangster film.

Last-minute rescue: Form of parallel montage, in which the pictures of the threatened groups are juxtaposed in shorter and shorter intervals with those of the rescuers rushing to save them. Typically, the rescue takes place at the last moment.

Montage: The skillful cutting and splicing of different shots to form a seamless film, but also the creative narrative technique of combining the different parts of the film into an artistic whole.

Nickelodeons: The first permanently established cinemas in America, which were named for the entrance price of a nickel.

One-reeler: One- to two-act film, of approximately 10 to 15 minute duration, that fit on one reel.

Point-of-view shot: Shot from the subjective perspective of a character.

Reverse shot editing: Two opposing individuals are shown in such a way that their actions appear in alternating fashion; this technique is used for the most part in dialogue scenes.

Shot: Smallest unit of film narration; a single phase picture or a sequence of phase pictures taken one after the other without changing the shot size or the camera perspective.

Shot scale: The chosen picture segment, differentiated into long shots, medium shots, close-ups, and extreme close-ups.

Showdown: Typical staging component of the western, in which the competing main counterparts meet in a final power struggle at the end of the film.

Film was never silent, though in the beginning it was not the word, but the music. Movie music is as old as the movies themselves. Even the Cinématogaphe Lumière was already accompanied by piano music, even if only in the beginning to drown out noise of the projector.

The accompanying music for the early program numbers on piano or with small-scale orchestras usually had no relationship to the pictures being shown. That changed dramatically when the film changed from being cheap entertainment at county fairs to middle-class entertainment. Camille Saint-Saëns was won over to collaborate on a prototype of the French film d'art *The Assassination of the Duke de Guise* (1908). Meanwhile, Ildebrando Pizetti was composing a "Sinfonia del Fuoco" for the burning of Carthage scene in Italy's first feature-length film, *Cabiria* (1914).

Inevitably, the Americans also followed. The Hollywood pioneer D. W. Griffith, of course, had no music composed to accompany his otherwise historically important, ground-breaking film *The Birth of a Nation* (1915); however, he knew how to heighten the effect of the emotionally charged epic through the creative selection and precise insertion of selections from opera overtures by Richard Wagner, Carl Maria von Weber, and Vincenzo Bellini.

The advantages of using music and picture together in harmony were quite evident, but use of original compositions remained the exception at first. The quality of accompanying music for silent films, for its part, depended on the repertoire and the improvisational talent of the accompanying musicians; the piano player, who was soon joined by a percussionist for sound effects, the organist at the Wurlitzer organ, which became commonplace after 1911, and finally the orchestral scores which emerged as the cinema blossomed. The accompanying music was never rigidly prescribed for the musicians. They availed themselves of film music libraries, archives where—drawing on the entire repertoire of the romantic era—appropriate musical numbers were available for every type of film: hectic music for the chase, idyllic music for love scenes, melancholy music to underscore fateful situations, and dramatic music to effectively announce

A silent-film pianist at work (1913).

Edmund Meisel was one of the most famous film composers of the 1920s. He wrote the music for Eisenstein's famous revolutionary film *Potemkin* (1925).

impending danger. The numbers were simply strung together during the showing and connected by improvised transitions.

The introduction of the sound film around 1927 had quite a variety of effects on film music. Naturally, the reproduction quality at first was inferior. Photographic sound-film, recording copied onto filmstrips, soon began to replace the needle pickup and the joining of gramophone and projector; the sound quality, however, did not approach that of the earlier live performances for quite some time. Since language, sound, and music in the early sound film were not separated but needed to be recorded simultaneously on one track, there was no possibility for mixing the sound track later on. Most film producers decided, therefore, to use either language or music in the new sound film. Thus the viewers of the first "all-talkies" had to do without the emotion-intensifying musical accompaniment (with exceptions such as Hitchcock's *Blackmail* [1929]), while film music broke new ground in the genre of the musical. Since dance and music here were at the center, original scores were now needed and had to be developed before the film, whereas accompanying music did not. Hollywood made use of proven material and artists from Broadway; in Germany, where the sound film operetta enjoyed success, hit composers followed suit.

At the same time, the film directors, who during the silent-film era were only able to have a very limited effect on the choice of accompanying music, discovered the possibilities of musical insertion. Hitchcock's *Blackmail* (1929), René Clair's *Under the Roofs of Paris* (1930), and Fritz Lang's *M* (1931) are among the first sound films in which music is not just background accompaniment but a valued, independent aesthetic element of the film. Over the course of film history, there has been repeated productive cooperation between directors and composers, especially in Europe: Sergei Eisenstein and Sergei Prokofiev (*Alexander Nevsky*, 1938), Bertolt Brecht and Hanns Eisler (*Kuhle Wampe*, 1931), Basil Wright and Benjamin Britten (*Night Mail*, 1936), Marcel Carné and Maurice Jaubert (*Daybreak*, 1939), Jean Renoir and Joseph Cosma (*Grand Illusion*, 1937), Federico Fellini and Nino Rota (all films, among them *La Strada*, 1954), and Peter Greenaway and Michael Nyman

The work of the composer first begins after the film is cut: The music is written according to the running time of the picture and is synchronized afterwards. The composer conducts the orchestra at the same time the film is playing, as he listens to the dialog through his headphones. The sound technician then mixes dialogue, sound, and music onto one soundtrack in the studio. This is copied as a photgraphic track onto the film strip. The London Symphony Orchestra during recording for a film in 1947.

(among others, *The Draughtman's Contract*, 1982).

In Hollywood, film music led a shadowy existence; relegated to being mere mood-makers, the composers were hardly ever mentioned in the credits. That changed first in the 1950s, when the industry discovered the marketing of film hits and title music as additional sources of income. The business of record licenses flourished especially during the 1960s, when the cinema lost its middle-class public to the competition of television, instead attracting to its dark halls the pop-music loving youth, with modern music films built around such stars as Elvis Presley and the Beatles. Since that time, almost all films with contemporary material have popular music composed for them, and the film music follows changes in style.

Even classical music is occasionally introduced, in American films particularly when the subject is the life story of a famous composer, such as Miloš Forman's homage to Mozart, *Amadeus* (1984). The Europeans reached back into music history without any direct thematic relationship, as when Luchino Visconti underscored *Death in Venice* (1970) with the work of Gustav Mahler, while Beethoven's string quartets dominate in Jean-Luc Godard's *First Name: Carmen* (1983).

Leading contemporary composers seldom write today for the cinema. The experimental documentary film *Koyaanisqatsi* (1976–1982) is one of the few exceptions, and a fascinating one because of its unusual montage of pictures with music by the founder of minimalist music Philip Glass. The sounds of the 20th century have been present in film music since the 1950s. Music that once only reached a small captive audience in the concert hall has become standard today in the mass cinema. The popular genre of the horror film with its agitated, panicky episodes would not be imaginable without the achievements of avant-garde compositions and sound effects. The musically most exciting horror and science fiction music of today comes from the avant-garde workshop of the Hollywood composer Jerry Goldsmith, who composed for famous genre films such as *The Omen* (1975), *Alien* (1979), and *Total Recall* (1990). Steven Spielberg's preferred composer John Williams is probably the only composer of today more successful than Goldsmith; his hymn-like melodies for almost all of the blockbusters from Spielberg's factory move up the charts to become million-sellers.

The Allies cultivated the image of the Germans as "brutish Huns" during World War I. In Cecil Hepworth's *The Outrage* (1915), a German soldier is killed in 1914 by the son of a woman whom he had raped during the Franco-Prussian War of 1870.

War and cinema

The First World War marked a turning point in the history of film. In the countries involved in the war, film production necessarily declined: artists and industrial workers went to the front and a number of factories producing raw materials for the film industry retooled in order to produce munitions. With Germany now their enemy, the French, Italians, and Danes, who had dominated the market, lost an important consumer. They lost their control of the global industry, even though the demand for films was increasing everywhere—in times of war the entertainment industry always booms.

The Americans, who had been expanding markedly since the first decade of the century into the international arena, filled the vacuum to assume the leading position among the film-producing nations in 1916, which it still maintains today. In isolated Germany, where no noteworthy film production had existed before the war, it was suddenly necessary to supply its 2,000 permanent movie theaters on its own with the desired diversion from the deprivations and dreariness of wartime. The number of movie making companies rose within a few years from 25 to 250. The semi-state-owned film concern Ufa (Universum-Film AG) was founded in 1917 and after the war was able to unload its films on the world market cheaply and without competition because of the high inflation rate. It rose to become the largest provider after the Hollywood studios.

In the end, the war also brought a previously hidden potential of the new mass medium to full bloom. The opposing camps used it skillfully for the purpose of military propaganda. Patriotic films were intended to promote support for the war and the civilian population's readiness to sacrifice. Each side outdid the other when it came to depicting the enemies as blood-thirsty beasts who slaughtered women and children, and glorifying their own heroism in light-hearted operettas about the war.

Film as a consumer product

While the Europeans attempted to utilize the mass appeal of the cinema for political purposes, the Americans primarily understood film as a consumer product, whose form and content had to subordinate itself entirely to the dictates of commercial exploitation. In Hollywood small production companies, vendors, and cinema owners banded together to form the three great studios Paramount-Publixs, Loew's (Metro-Goldwyn-Mayer), and First National, which took over the top positions in the market. Right behind them were the "Little Five," Universal, Fox Film Corp., the Producer Distribution Corp., the Film Booking Office, and Warner Brothers. Thanks to this

Only a few weeks before the end of the war Chaplin made the first film critical of it in the form of a satire. *Shoulder Arms* (1918) sheds a very human light on life in the trenches and communicates a realistic picture of the war.

Fan magazines already helped promote new stars in the second decade of the century.

concentration, the film industry rose to be the third most important sales branch in the United States by 1930. The capital for this enormous expansion was provided by New York banks, which in the 1920's had acquired the majority of stock of all the large studios, and finally took over decision-making power in the studios on artistic matters, as well.

To be successful on the world market, a product had to be standardized according to market requirements. In the eyes of the banking experts, who as supervisors soon controlled all decisions in the various stages of film production, the following ingredients led to the success of a film and determined its sales worth, its so-called "box-office value": famous stars ("star value"), elaborate sets and prestige-enhancing pub-lication of the production costs ("production value"), and popular content, which, if possible, had already proven successful as a play or novel ("story value"). The studios built up their filmstars through tar-geted advertising cam-paigns and committed themselves to successful character clichés. The Hollywood directors from the 1920's that are most often named in film histories, such as Ernst Lubitsch, Cecil B. De Mille, and Charles Chaplin, in reality

Mary Pickford was the first actress who was intentionally made into a star. From then on, future idols were selected according to the following criteria: they had to fit into a clear-cut type whose character was reflected in their looks, have an unmistakable, photogenic face, and lots of charisma. Like Mary Pickford the preferred female stars were first and foremost faithful, sweet girls who found their fulfillment in a man.

represented exceptions who could afford a certain degree of independence because of their extraordinary success, as long as they were not constantly sparring with their producers, such as Erich von Stroheim or Robert Flaherty did, because of their artistic inflexibility. Film production in the 1920's was actually dominated for the most part by average directors who were severely restricted and who were not even allowed to make the last cut in their films. Even today, the right of the last cut is only granted to a very few extraordinary directors. The studios increasingly specialized in genres such as westerns, gangster films, melodramas, societal comedies, and historical films, but in reality their stylized sets merely covered superficial variations of a tried-and-true success formula.

A distinction was also made between expensively produced prestige films, the A pictures, usually with budgets exceeding $500,000, and the cheaper

Rudolph Valentino created the Latin lover type and, along with Douglas Fairbanks, was the most beloved star of his day, though he played the leading role in only six films before his early death in 1926. Publicity about the stars' supposed private lives was already a standard part of advertising campaigns. But as more and more scandals were reported in the press, the movies themselves became morally suspect, and so the film industry conceded to government censorship by the newly created Hays Office for voluntary self-regulation. Scene from Valentino's last film *The Son of the Sheik* (1926).

The large studios purposefully brought the best forces of the European cinema to Hollywood even during the silent-film era. One of the most lucrative imports was the German Ernst Lubitsch (1892–1947), whose extraordinary talent as a director had drawn attention to such brilliant and erotically titillating films as his melodrama *Madame Dubarry* (1919).

Erich von Stroheim (1885–1957), who was admired by Eisenstein, Renoir, and Cocteau as the greatest cinematic genius of his day, was among the first prominent victims of the studio system. He was not able to edit his brilliant material to commercial standards. Only his film debut *Blind Husbands* (1918) appeared in theaters unscathed. His extremely long masterpieces, including *Greed* (1924), were reduced to typical feature-film length; Stroheim was replaced as director of every film he started thereafter before their completion.

French burlesque films provided the prototype for American slapstick.

B pictures, which were forced upon the movie theaters within the framework of the so-called block-booking system in packages with the box office smash hits.

Slapstick

In Hollywood, during the early years of the silent film, one genre dominated: the comedy. Griffith protégé Mack Sennett (1884–1960) is called the father of slapstick, though he himself attributed his inspiration to French burlesque film. In his slapstick factory he produced one-reeler grotesques in assembly-line fashion according to the principle of the Italian *commedia dell'arte*. The plot's coarse comedy was improvised along the lines of a general design. A cake fight formed the highpoint; a breakneck chase in precise and rapid cuts led to the furious finale. Invariably involved were a chaotic group of policemen, the beloved "Keystone Kops," beautiful girls, and simple-minded scapegoats who survived the most awful catastrophes. Aggression, malicious glee, and anarchical desire for the final orgies of destruction determined the sequencing of one-after-the-other gags, with little value placed on narrative probability. With specific objectives in mind, Sennett perfected the art of slapstick in over 500 short films, tested the comical effects of increasing film speed and reversing direction,

Mack Sennett was very responsive to public reactions. He discovered, for example, that a picture of scantily clad bathing beauties had great advertising value for his films, and in 1915 introduced the "Bathing Beauties" into his films as the second permanent troupe next to his chaotic group of police, the "Keystone Kops."

and freed the camera, which had to be just as mobile as the comedians themselves, from the stationary position of a theater audience.

The great American film comedians

In the 1920's the most successful stars of slapstick gradually moved on to produce feature-length comedies. Their trademarks were the unique comic personalities, mostly social outsiders who confronted life's big and small catastrophes in their typical, unchanging styles. Charlie Chaplin's humorous-sentimental tramp in the worn-out walking suit of an important man about town, Buster Keaton's unshakable "stoneface," Harold Lloyd's (1893–1971) clumsy boy next door, and the dissimilar pair Laurel & Hardy refined crude slapstick into a masterful visual comedic art.

The work habits of the film comedians is worth noting. They almost all came from vaudeville or variety-show backgrounds and had learned the craft of film from Mack Sennett or his competitor, the independent producer Hal Roach. Without fixed film scripts, they worked out their stories while improvising on the set, starting sometimes with just one prop, a gag, or a little everyday scene that they had observed somewhere. This painstaking approach dragged out the filming time to uncontrollably

Charles Chaplin (1889–1977) gradually refined his rather coarse and lewd little tramp into a sympathetic underdog, who made his way through life with humor and feeling, but still never managed to get a foot in the door of bourgeois society. Characteristic of Chaplin's films is the combination of comedy and social tragedy, combined with a clear political engagement and an increasing tendency toward pathos and sentimentality. Among his greatest silent-film successes were *The Kid* (1920) and the pioneer fairy tale *The Gold Rush* (1925).

Compared to Chaplin, Buster Keaton's (1895–1966) "stone-face" is a rather unsociable character, who unflaggingly casts himself into the apparently hopeless struggle with the material world. Whether in a bind with an abandoned steamship in *The Navigator* (1924), a locomotive in *The General* (1927), or a film camera in *The Cameraman* (1928): Keaton depicts people in the machine age with bizarre humor often bordering on surrealism without once cracking a smile.

The most typically American figure was developed by Harold Lloyd. His boy-next-door with thick glasses and straw hat was an average small-town resident who endured unimaginable adventures, only to unexpectedly become a hero. At the highpoint of his "thrill comedies" he finds himself hanging from a skyscraper at a dizzying height, for example, as in his perhaps most famous stunt in *Safety Last* from 1923.

In 1927, Stan Laurel (1890–1965) and Oliver Hardy (1892–1957) began one of the most fruitful partnerships in film history. Their comedy grew out of the confrontation between the dissimilar partners: the fat one against the skinny one, the hopelessly suffering Papa Olli against a childishly mischievous Stan. Like a pair of lovers bound in marriage, they fight incessantly and yet cannot exist without each other.

great lengths and made the success of the film, at least in the eyes of the financial backers, unpredictable. Chaplin, for example, was of the opinion that "A person ought to work on a good film for at least a year," and without batting an eye, used over 30,000 feet of raw film for a movie that in the end would be just 2,000 feet long. Only financially independent stars could afford such production conditions, while in the market-leading studios the New York supervisors were already setting the tone with their standardized production guidelines.

In the end, the inevitable integration into the large studios' production machinery proved much more detrimental to silent-film comedians than the introduction of sound films. In the late 1920's, for example, Keaton relinquished his independence and became an MGM star, of course with the expectation that he would work in line with a set film script. His spontaneity suffered under the constraints of rigid studio work, and although his first sound films still became box-office successes, he could no longer make the artistic connection to his silent-film success. Laurel & Hardy suffered a similar fate when Twentieth Century Fox and MGM joined together in the 1940's. They lost their freshness and became increasingly outdated. Chaplin, on the other hand, warded off the threatening dependency in 1919 by founding United Artists along with other stars; their explicit goal was to finance "quality films" by

The famous founders of United Artists: Douglas Fairbanks, Mary Pickford, Charles Chaplin, and D. W. Griffith.

independent producers who did not want to subject themselves to the dictates of the large studios.

The European avant-garde

The First World War had severely restricted the international influence of the European film nations. Hollywood had controlled the world market almost unchallenged since the 1920's. The sales of the large American studios were so astronomical that their directors controlled the largest production budgets in the world and could invest staggering sums in stars, costumes, sets, and special effects. Under these circumstances, it was decidedly more feasible for the European film industry to buy and distribute American films than to produce their own. Great companies like Pathé and Gaumont concentrated on the rental business. During the mid-1920's only about 10 movies a year were made in Italy, and in 1926 just 5 % of the films shown in England were produced there, while in France the figure was about 10%. However, the decline of the former industry leaders made room for a new generation of film artists.

When World War I severely reduced the importation of foreign films, neutral Sweden's film industry energetically promoted the development of its own directing talents Mauritz Stiller (1883–1928) and Victor Sjöström (1879–1960). Sjöström's films drew international attention because of their extraordinary combination of the depiction of nature and the emotional world of their characters. In *Terje Vigen* (1916), the fisherman Terje wrangles with the beauty and horror of nature after the death of his family. Like Sjostrom, Stiller, a master of ironic comedy, was also brought to Hollywood in the early 1920's. He brought along Greta Garbo (1905–1990), who first attracted international attention in his film *Gösta Berling* (1924, left).

Small companies attempted to conquer their own niche with avant-garde productions. Fascinated by Griffith's aesthetic advances, the young artists wanted to create alternatives to Hollywood's standardized mass productions. Educated people became increasingly interested in the cinema. In many European countries film clubs, such as the London Film Society or The Paris Ciné-Club, set up special cinemas for avant-garde film, organized lectures, exhibitions, and public discussions, and prompted lively theoretical debate in the early film magazines.

A typical Impressionist effect: In Dimitri Kirsanov's *Ménilmontant*, (1926) the heroine's tumultuous feelings are given expression by the river, which is superimposed on a close-up of her face.

French Impressionism

The French "cinéasts" were especially successful in creating enthusiasm among a specialized intellectual public for the "seventh art." A group of directors, Louis Delluc, Germaine Dulac, Abel Gance, Marcel L'Herbier, and Jean Ebstein, affiliated themselves with impressionistic cinematic art and presented their theories in poetic essays. Art, they postulated, conveys no truths but merely experiences. The personal view of the artist and "emotions instead of stories" should comprise the core of a film and allow it to become the "poetic expression of the soul." In 1918 Delluc defined the decisive quality that differentiates a film picture from the pictured object with the concept *photogénie*. Picturing the object, wrote Delluc, lends an object new meaning by opening the viewer to a new perspective of it through the eyes of the person filming.

In practice the Impressionist directors at first concentrated on the picture itself. By using optical tricks, they attempted to illustrate the impressions of the film characters: Dreams, memories, visions, and thoughts. They made shots using a distorted mirror, put excerpts of pictures through filters, or divided

For Marcel L'Herbier's *The New Enchantment* (1924), part of the stage set was designed by the notable architect R. Mallet-Stevens.

the frame into smaller individual pictures. They emphasized the subjectivity of the perspective with the "subjective camera," that is, through extreme perspectives, tilted picture formats, and camera movements that showed us the scene through the eyes of the characters. The Impressionists attached the greatest importance to the *mise-en-scène*, i. e., to all the elements which make up the staging of a film picture. They encouraged untheatrical and reserved acting, and used lighting effectively to illuminate spaces that were in part created by contemporary painters and architects in cubist or art deco style. After 1923 the Impressionists freed themselves from their fixation on the picture and camera focus and, inspired by Griffith's daring montages, experimented with rhythmical cut sequences. For example, especially quick cut sequences were

Abel Gance's (1889–1981) historical epic "Napoleon" (1927) is one of the most ambitious film projects of the 1920's. In this monumental film of originally 12 hours' playing time Gance employed the latest film techniques with virtuosity: A distorting mirror, double exposures, rapid cut sequences, and very free use of the hand-held camera, which he mounted on the back of a horse or had thrown back and forth during a snowball fight. The film is also famous for its wide-format panorama shots. To project them, three screens had to be set up next to each other, which served as a tableau for the simultaneous projection of three frames as a kind of triptych. The costly restoration of the mutilated film for the premiere took the restorers of the *Cinémathèque*

supposed to make the inner tumult of the protagonist imaginable.

Française 10 years, from 1969 to 1979.

Cinéma pur

In search of the pure art of the film, a few avant-garde film makers turned away from stories and content entirely and embarked on the radical path of

cinéma pur, also known as "absolute film." The proponents of the graphically-abstract approach originally intended to free film not only from all dramatic elements, but also from photographical-documentary aspects, and defined film as the play of rhythmically ordered colors and forms, as "paintings in time." In 1924 the painter Fernand Léger created one of the first abstract movies on the basis of photographical material: *Le Ballet méchanique* was a rhythmical montage of pictures of a woman trudging up a staircase, dancing kitchen utensils, and a cubist Chaplin doll. One of the most important movies of the *cinéma pur* is René Clair's (1898–1981) Dada-influenced *Entr'acte* (1924). Supposedly, the director compiled the fantastic-surreal pictures that make up this crazy collage soley according to the "movement value" of the images, which was decisive for the rhythm of the film.

The most important German representative of the absolute film was Walter Ruttmann (1887–1941). In the movies *Opus I–IV*, made between 1921 and 1924, he experimented with pure graphic, abstract forms (see above); however, his most famous film was *Berlin: Symphony of a Big City* (1927), a radical experiment with movement and rhythm composed of documentary pictures of contemporary Berlin.

Surrealistic film

The avant-garde film of the 1920's reached its apex, and the greatest public attention, with the films of Luis Buñuel (1900–1983). Together with the artist Salvador Dalí, he staged shocking images and, influenced by the rising interest in psychoanalysis, arranged them in alogical, dreamlike series of associations. In *An Andalusian Dog* (1928) pictures of a love story rise up as if from the subconscious of the protagonist. A man cuts the eye of a young girl with a razor in a close-up. Another sequence of pictures shows priests, melons, pianos, and donkey carcasses,

One of the most famous and most quoted scenes in the history of film from *An Andalusian Dog*. The film quickly became an extraordinary public success in 1928. After its premier it ran for nine consecutive months to a full house.

which are tied to a young man and prevent him from reaching a girl. Buñuel made an even more shocking and

provoking attack on middle-class values with his first sound film *The Golden Age* (1930). With this blasphemous attack on all societal powers of authority, at the climax of which Christ appears as the last survivor of a sadistic orgy, Buñuel rebelled against sexual and political repression of every kind.

The surrealistic movement, which included the likes of the American photographer Man Ray with his film *L'Etoile de Mer* (1929) and Germaine Dulac's *La Coquille et le Clergyman* (1927), splintered between left and right extremism in the 1930's. They and their films, however, exercised a strong influence on the re-direction of European cinema following the Second World War, particularly on the directors Federico Fellini, Pier Paolo Pasolini, Jean Cocteau, Carlos Saura, and Bernardo Bertolucci.

In the end, those possessed by love lost the desperate battle against faddish sexual cultural rules; the heroine sucks on the big toe of a statue in frustration. The Buñuel-Dalí team's second film, *The Golden Age*, shocked the middle-class and clerical world to a degree that is hardly comprehensible today and was banned shortly after its premier.

German expressionism

The majority of German film productions during World War I consisted of entertainment films—comedies, melodramas, and detective films—that scarcely differed from the standard fare world-wide. International attention was first roused by attempts to create an art film in the expressionist style that was popular in the contemporary art scene. The undertaking was begun along general lines in the late 1910's by several artists, and was enthusiastically supported by the large film companies. They speculated that an aesthetic novelty could pave the way for a re-invigorated German export effort and would win a new, middle-class audience for the new

The most successful expressionist film, Robert Wiene's (1881–1938) *The Cabinet of Dr. Caligari,* (1919) was planned as a box-office success for the artistically-minded public. It was accompanied by a refined advertising campaign and premiered in large movie palaces in order to underscore its market uniqueness, and simultaneously to secure it the necessary media attention.

Expressionism discovered light and shadow as formal dimensions. *Nosferatu the Vampire* (1922) by Friedrich Wilhelm Murnau (1888–1931) is only partially within the movement, but is clearly influenced by it. In this first vampire film, Murnau rejected typically stylized decorations, and derived an oppressive atmosphere of the eerie from nature and reality through specific camera techniques and skillful use of lighting. Other important films of Murnau are *The Last Laugh* (1924) and his famous filming of Goethe's *Faust* (1926).

medium at home as well. In the theater and in painting, expressionism had established itself at the start of the century as a reaction to realism. Expressionistic artists wanted to portray the inner reality of emotions rather than the outer appearance of reality. The spirit of the times was still very much imbued with the war and its aftermath in the early 1920's, leading to a plethora of foreboding, fantastic motifs and individuals who are powerless against superhuman beings, merciless twists of fate, or dark personal instincts populating the screen of the Expressionist films. This choice of material was either interpreted as an escape from the oppressive reality of the post-war period into a horror enraptured Romanticism, or as a predilection of the next, even more horrific war.

German expressionism owes its success above all to its artificial sets and staging. Expressionistic films came very close to contemporary theater; they were created in front of rather than with the camera. The actors wore their hearts on their sleeves and acted with exaggerated movements, which make them seem like the extreme gestures of silent films to the casual observer today. But these stilted actions formed an organic whole in the context of the contrasting environment of flatly painted sets. Expressionistic set designers created inspired sets that reflected the inner lives of the acting characters in their distorted proportions. The stage sets were draped in expressive light and shadow effects, while unusual rotations of axis and extreme camera angles imbued them with eerie and symbolic meaning.

Despite the great international success of *The Cabinet of Dr. Caligari* (1919), the first expressionist film, the artificial style could not maintain itself in the long run; however, its influence on the development of the horror and gangster genres of the 1930's is undeniable. After a short blossoming, expressionism gave way to the *Neue Sachlichkeit* (New Objectivity), a stylistic trend which, in contrast to its

forerunner, was dedicated to the depiction and critical observation of social reality.

The Soviet revolutionary film

In the USSR right after the Revolution, young artists set to work to create a socialist art. As in the theater, literature, the fine arts, and photography, the filmmakers experimented using the ideas of futurism and of constructivism as a starting point. Strong impetus for the rise of avant-garde film, which was first promoted by the National Education Commission, came of course from Hollywood. The Soviet filmmakers admired in Griffith above all— *Intolerance* was shown in 1919 in Moscow to great cheers—his sense of heightening tempo and contrasts, along with his montage technique. The experimental further development of montage was to

Beside Murnau, Fritz Lang (1890–1976) is the only outstanding expressionist director. *Der müde Tod* (1921) – variably released in the U.S. as *Between Two Worlds* and *Beyond the Wall* and in the UK as *Destiny* – and *Dr. Mabuse the Gambler* (1922), also known simply as *Dr. Mabuse* or *The Fatal Passions*, takes place in decidedly artificial stage settings and makes use of expressionist lighting. His master-piece, *Metropolis* (1926), stands out for its large-scale construction, brilliantly composed play of light and shadow, rhythmic cuts and impressive mass scenes. The science fiction story, however, was criticized because of its proximity to fascist thinking—the idealization of a bond between the oppressed working class and an elite class of leaders. Lang distanced himself from the National Socialists, who admired his film *Die Nibelungen* (1924), and fled to France in 1933.

The Soviet leadership recognized the value of the new medium for propaganda from the start. "The art of film is for us the most important of all the arts," Lenin declared, and a public resolution on the cinema recommended its transformation to a "genuine and powerful weapon for the enlightenment of the working class and the broad masses of the people, and to one of the most important means in the holy struggle of the proletariat away from the narrow path of bourgeois art." Poster from Alexander Dovzhenko's film *Earth* (1930, sometimes known as *Soil*), which deals with the conflict between the tractor operators of the Kolchos and the collectivist farmers in the reform phase of the early Soviet Union.

Already in 1918 "Agit" trains were introduced, which were supposed to reach to the most remote regions of the Soviet Union and provide a cinema program which would build up the morale of the hard-pressed Red Army and agitate the predominantly illiterate population for socialism.

become a most important characteristic of Russian avant-garde film.

Then, however, the young filmmakers argued with one another about the political implications of the formal progress. The specific form of the Hollywood film, as they criticized it, functioned as a medium of ideological messages. The montage technique of the "invisible cut" and the typical dramatic tension of the stagings of the "American dream" they explained as affirmative aesthetics which was stamped with capitalistic values and manipulated rather than activated the audience. The recently developing socialist aesthetic on the other hand was supposed to challenge the viewer to think along and reflect the reality of societal relationships.

Sergei M. Eisenstein (1898–1948) studied architecture, took up the side of the Red army in the civil war, and worked at the Proletkult Theater before he made the first of his aesthetically innovative revolution films in 1923. In 1929 Eisenstein traveled abroad on official assignment, presumably to research new sound-film techniques. Film projects in Hollywood and Mexico failed and even after his return to the Soviet Union in 1933 he was criticized as a formalist artist and was not able to connect with his earlier successes.

Montage experiments

Griffith employed the new technique of montage primarily for heightening the dramatic tension effectively. In his cross cutting he confronted sharp contrasts as, for example, poverty and wealth, without however indicating the causes of the conflict. But it was the Russian avant-garde filmmakers who used such a montage technique in the manner of a dialectical argumentation of the montage. At the film college in Moscow a circle of young filmmakers gathered under the leadership of Lev Kuleshov (1899–1970), who attempted to find theoretical and experimental ways in which abstract thoughts could e portrayed in the silent film. The primary thesis was hat in the cinema the cut ranks ahead of the picture ontent, therefore meaning is communicated through montage rather than through the *mise-en-scène*. "With montage," according to Kuleshov, "one can destroy, epair, or entirely reformulate one's material."

He offered the proof for this fact with a famous xperiment, which became known as the Kuleshov ffect. He combined copies of a single, almost xpressionless close-up of an actor in a filmstrip lternating with the picture of a dead woman, of a late of soup, and of a girl at play. The public praised he differentiated means of expression of the actor, whom one believes to have discovered in his picture. 'he viewer, so Kuleshov concluded, therefore under-tands precisely what the montage suggests to him.

'rom the "montage of attractions" to intellectual montage"

mong the most important representatives of the novement, the feature film directors Sergei M. isenstein (1898–1948) and Vsevolod Pudovkin 1893–1953) are to be listed along with the docu-nentary film maker Dziga Vertov (1896–1954). They howed in their films the multiple possibilities of inematic montage and stand within the montage novement for two opposing tendencies. Eisenstein irst promoted the "montage of attractions" and the collision montage," a quick sequence of highly motionally charged pictures, which in a shocking nanner collide with one another in order to shake he viewer and to bring him to new realizations. In he final sequence of his first film *Strike* (1924) he ut pictures of the murder of the strikers against loody frames from a slaughter house. The film eceived international attention and brought isenstein the task of making a film for the 20th nniversary of the Revolution of 1905. In *The Battleship Potemkin* (1925), more familiar in the United States as simply *Potemkin*, Eisenstein

The goal of the artistic montage of Dziga Vertov was to catch life unawares in his insigni-ficant details with the cinematic eye. The documentary filmmaker named the feature film "Cinema nicotine," and rejected it because it stunted perception of social and political reality like a drug. Instead, between 1922 and 1925 he produced a new form of the weekly newsreel, the Kino-Pravda (Cinematic Truth), for which he composed documentary film material, which he had taken at different places and at different times, for party mes-sages. Among his most important films is *Man With a Movie Camera* (1929), also shown in the U.S. as *Moscow Today* and *Living Russia or the Man With the Camera*, a fireworks of montage and trick effects. Vertov makes the camera itself the protagonist and uncov-ers the fine differences between reality and filmed reality.

In the famous "staircase sequence" from *Potemkin* czarist soldiers slaughter peaceful demonstrators on the open steppes of Odessa. Eisenstein emphasizes the moral superiority of the people by means of rhythmic and contrasting montage. The Czarists march down the stairs, while the people force their way up with revolutionary elan. The inevitable confrontation culminated in quick cuts between the brutal faces and boots of the uniformed soldiers and pictures of the individual need of wounded and murdered mothers and children.

developed his montage technique further. An example for the "rhythmical montage" of the film: in faster and faster cuts Eisenstein shows progressively larger pictures of the rotating wheels of a tank and creates thereby a impressive metaphor for socialist progress.

Vsevolod Pudovkin also knew how to employ this "intellectual montage," i. e., the argumentative composition of film pictures. In his historical drama *The End of St. Petersburg* (1927) he contrasted pictures of hectically speculating stock brokers with horror pictures from the trenches. The attached insert title "What are we dying for?" is just a rhetorical question, which already appears to have been answered in the previous montage. All together Pudovkin's films are much closer to the classical narrative cinema *à la* Hollywood, which was also very popular with the Russian public, than the unconventional experiments of Eisenstein. A comparison between *Mother* (1926), the exceptionally successful first feature film of Pudovkin, and *Potemkin* illustrates the contrasts of the two most important filmmakers of the Revolution. Pudovkin's linearly narrated film is based on an invented story and shows psychologically conceived heroic characters, who were portrayed by the country's prominent actors. Eisenstein told the story of the revolt in Odessa in the form of a rhythmical collage of pictures, made the masses the hero, and had the characters who were reduced to stereotypes played by non-professionals. Montage served Pudovkin as a means to illustrate feelings and had the goal of awakening the emotions of the viewers rather than provoking them to be reflective: the images of protesting factory workers alternates with rays of sunlight, which tear through the walls of clouds, and ice floes breaking up. These images form a metaphor of revolutionary hope. Stalinist totalitarianism finally put a halt to the desire for experimentation of the Soviet avant-garde. At the end of the 1920's the party leadership increasingly took offense at formalism in the cinema and instead imposed the reorientation toward the doctrine of social realism, which led the Soviet cinema into an artistic dead-end street. Films were supposed to offer either light entertainment or encourage the formation of the socialist state.

Contemporary art movements which influenced the avant-garde film:

Impressionism (from 1870): French art movement, whose representatives were interested exclusively in the accidental, momentary, external forms of viewing the world. Light, atmosphere, movement and dissipating lines form the specific formal elements.

Cubism (from 1900): Artistic direction which moves the objects represented back to geometrical figures and shows them in their three-dimensionality, i. e., in the facets of different views and compartmentalized next to one another. The Cubist removes himself further and further from concrete objectivity and prepares the way for the abstract painting of the 20th century.

Expressionism (from 1905): Expressionist artists were interested in making the expression of the inner soul visible. Their pictures often show dreary basic moods which, at the turn of the century, mirrored the doubt-filled picture of humanity. Specific formal means are elementary, reduced forms in distorted proportions and a free, partially aggressive application of color.

Futurism (from 1909): Central focus of the Italian art movement was to express the spirit of the modern technical world in the visual realization of movement. Typical motifs are people moving in opposite directions, galloping horses, stamping machines, automobiles traveling at high speed. The sensation of motion is created by repetition of the objects and abstract lines.

Dadaism (from 1916): With the horrors of the First World War the Dadaists questioned fundamentally all aesthetic and contextual rules of form and established their provocative anti-art on the principle of chance. Thus sound poems without meaning, concerts of noise, picture and material collages developed.

Surrealism (from 1920): The goal of the surrealistic artist was to connect the real world and the world of dreams in an extreme reality, which uncovers other levels of consciousness and creates meaning through visions. The veristic trend show realistic objects in totally absurd combinations, absolute surrealism chooses an abstract treatment of the themes of dream and the subconscious.

Constructivism: Constructivism was the official art movement of the Russian Revolution between 1917 and 1921. The determining creative principles are distinct, unambiguous, however mostly non-representational forms, whose clear, constructive design should reflect the completely and meaningfully formed, man-created world.

Art Deco (1920–1940): Commercial artistic trend, whose strictly decorative forms reflected the world of industrial manufacturing processes as "machine aesthetics."

Economic crisis changes the world

On October 25, 1929, "Black Friday," the New York stock market crash marked the beginning of the world-wide economic crisis. For an entire decade, the Depression dominated the social and political climate. It caused millions of people to lose their jobs, banks to collapse, and international productivity to sink by over 50 percent, while inflation weakened buying power and, therefore, trade. As a result of this economic decline, the gap between rich and poor increased throughout the world, and social conflicts intensified. In France and Spain, for a short period of time in the 1930s, leftist peoples' front organizations took over the government and brought about comprehensive social reforms. In America, the newly-elected Democratic President Franklin D. Roosevelt introduced a period of liberalization and a turn toward a social principle of state with his "New Deal" policies.

At the same time, fascism was spreading. Long before the fascist General Franco emerged as victor from the Spanish Civil War in 1939, Mussolini had already seized power in Italy in 1922, and since the beginning of the 1930s the Japanese government had been taking a decided turn to the right with its increasingly imperialistic politics. In Germany as well, political polarization ended the brief blossoming of democracy and brought Hitler and the National Socialists to power. Eventually, they would cast the world into the catastrophic Second World War.

The victory march of the sound film

At first, the film industry was comparatively little affected by the world economic crisis. The cinema offered people the most accessible and most harmless form of diversion. Warner Brothers, which had expanded tremendously at the end of the 1920s and was therefore highly in debt, caused a sensation in the market in 1927 with its first sound film, *The Jazz Singer*, which enthralled the public and brought ı enormous profits. The other studios inevitably ollowed along. In 1929, over half of the approximately 20,500 American cinemas had already witched over to sound film projection, while the innovation also began to establish itself in major uropean cities.

It might seem surprising that the cinema had to ırn 30 years old before it learned to speak, specially since the discovery of the phonograph had receded the discovery of the Kinetograph. Attempts) bring sound to moving pictures are, in the final nalysis, as old as the cinema itself. From the eginning, moving pictures had been accompanied y commentators, harmonium players, or entire rchestras. Many cinemas had at their disposal a rand array of noise machines that were used "live" uring the film. Already around the turn of the entury, people had tried to increase the ttractiveness of "moving photographs" through nechanical sound reproduction. Between 1904 and 913, in some performances, film was joined nechanically with gramophone sound. The ynchronization, of course, left much to be desired, ecause only a maximum of five minutes of sound fit n a platter, and sound from a gramophone could nly be introduced into small theaters. The early ound pictures disappeared again from the screen ith the introduction of full-length films and of the

great movie houses. Warner Brothers' Vitaphone system, which finally helped the sound film make its breakthrough, continued to work on the principle of sound-on-disc, and improved sound from the platter with an electromagnetic pickup. Soon, however, the

1941
Bombing of Pearl Harbor leads America into the war

1942
Erecting of extermination camps in Auschwitz, Maidanek, Bergen-Belsen, etc.

1944
Otto Hahn receives the Nobel Peace Prize for the first fission of neutrons

Program from the Phono-Cinéma-Théâter ca. 1900, announcing "speaking" films with the theatrical star Sarah Bernhardt, among others.

In 1926, the first film with musical accompaniment using the Vitaphone process appeared with *Don Juan*; however, there was still no dialogue in this film.

The photographic soundtrack translates pitch and volume in regular patterns of light. This process, which made it technically easier to record sound quickly, established itself to the disadvantage of sound from needle pickup. In the 1950s, work was also begun on magnetic soundtracks, which provided a considerably improved sound quality, but were much more subject to interruptions. In the meantime, the reproductive quality of photographic sound had been optimized with the result that hardly any more magnetic copies were made.

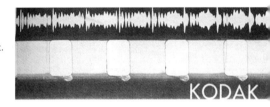

photographic sound film developed in Germany forced all other sound film systems from the marketplace. In this process, sound is transformed electrically into light waves and copied directly onto the film strip. Synchronization of sound and picture needed no longer be disrupted by breaks in the film.

Adaptation difficulties

The late and sluggish adoption of the sound film can best be explained by the studios' economic reservations. The necessary retooling of the studios and cinemas was associated with high costs, which could be absorbed only to a very limited degree by ticket sales because of the economic crisis. People in the film industry rightly feared that silent-film stars, who had been promoted at great cost, would not be able to speak and sing adequately and would therefore lose their box-office appeal. And one thing was for sure: Sound films could not, of course, be marketed internationally as easily as silent films, with their easily exchangeable commentary. In reality, the changeover to the sound film left enough playing room for the lagging European producers to rebuild their film industry and to achieve a certain independence in the short run. The British, 95 percent of whose market after 1916 was in American hands, made 225 films in 1936 and became the second-largest provider of films on the international market. This enormous advance came about through the introduction of a quota system for British-made productions and was supported by the buildup of a production system modeled on that of the Hollywood studios. Meanwhile, on the other hand, the

"Wait a minute! Wait a minute! You ain't heard nothing yet!" are the first two lines to be spoken in a sound film. They brought the public to spontaneous applause. *The Jazz Singer*, still not completely synchronized, ended the silent film era. The first "hundred-percent speaking film" was *The Lights of New York* (1928).

consequences of the worldwide economic crisis had caught up with Hollywood and sent its studios, almost without exception, into financial difficulties as a result of the changeover. Bankruptcies and mergers changed the market. In the end, five large, new

studios, the "Majors" of Paramount, MGM, Warner Bros., Twentieth Century Fox, and RKO, and three small ones, the "Minors" of Universal, Columbia, and United Artists, were able to bring almost all of the production, leasing, and other types of theater chains under their control. The market leaders lent each other artistic and technical personnel, dividing up the U.S. market among themselves. With such extraordinary cooperation, the new cartel successfully forced independent companies from the market and were able from that point on to maintain a monopoly in the film industry.

Chaplin was the only one who, in 1936, could afford to film without spoken text. The little tramp, who, by the way, appears for the last time in *Modern Times*, mimics a singing waiter, but the text consists only of nonsense words. The social satire castigated exaggerated rationalization in the industrial age and the increasing mechanization of life.

The artistic challenge

In light of the great economic challenges surrounding the introduction of the sound film, aesthetic objections against the new technology

played, at best, a secondary role. Some filmmakers, of course, prophesied the decline of cinematic art as it had been highly developed in the silent film. First of all, the sound film placed very concrete limitations on cameramen and actors. The complicated sound-film techniques

Norma Talmadge (1897–1957), along with John Gilbert, who was ridiculed because of his high, feminine voice, was one of the most famous victims of the sound film. After hundreds of successful silent films, her first entry into the sound film *DuBarry—Women of Passion* disclosed the fact that she was only able to speak in slang and ended her career abruptly.

71

So that sound films could also be sold on the international market, many were filmed in multiple versions using German, English, and French actors, as in the catastrophe film *Atlantic* (1929) that was produced for England and Germany. As a rule today, multiple versions are seldom filmed; typically, in their place, subtitles and foreign language synchronization are added later.

bound the camera, which had become mobile, back to a fixed position, and the actors were also not allowed to move far away from the microphone. Instead of using original sites, films could now be made only in studios. Also, people were afraid that the painstakingly created visual world, and the wealth of associations pictured in the silent medium, would be rendered superfluous by the introduction of sound. The film theoretician Rudolf Arnheim took the position, in his essay "Film as Art" (1932), that the structural freedom that made the film into art was a direct outgrowth of its limitations. Art, postulated Arnheim, comes to exist exclusively through the deviation of the work from reality. Since sound brought the film closer to reality, he bemoaned the "strangulation of a beautiful, hope-filled art form." Directors eager to experiment nonetheless got immediately down to the business of developing the new artistic possibilities attendant to the sound film.

The filmmakers of the Russian Revolution greeted sound as additional material for their dialectical montage artworks and as a way around the acute restrictions of the medium. They argued for a contrapuntal introduction of sound. Sounds and dialogs, proposed Pudovkin and Eisenstein in their legendary manifesto on the sound film, could enter into contradictory or even asynchronous relationship with visual montage elements. After the first technical problems of the sound film had been conquered with microphones mounted on long arms and the sound-isolated camera finally movable again, even the skeptics recognized that innovatively used sound could enhance the art of film-making. "Off-screen" sound, the source of which is not to be seen in the picture, could for example create a realistic atmosphere, conveying information which could go far beyond the picture content; the use of sound cuts, mixing, and post-synchronization helped overcome the limitations that had been imposed upon sound before.

Film and reality

The aesthetic changes which the sound film brought with it were less significant than the technical and organizational ones. The most important stylistic elements, such as montage, camera movement, *mise-en-scène*, trick techniques, and the narrative strategies typical of the classical Hollywood films, were already present in the great silent films. After a short phase, during which sound filmmakers became satisfied with picturing speaking actors, these elements again belonged among the determining structural means. Film became more natural through sound. The illusion of reality in the motion and sound pictures had come to supersede by far that of any other medium. It is possible that this great similarity between film perception and perception of reality is the reason for the extraordinary popularity of the cinema, as the film semiotician Christian Metz tried to explain in 1972. In any case, the movie industry ultimately devoted itself, with the discovery of sound film, almost exclusively to the production of naturalistic narrative films with the exception, of course, of cartoons.

Abstract and experimental films, though they had been promoted totally by commercially-minded producers during the 1920s, were made from that point on only as reactions to the products of the film industry or, at best, on its periphery. But, although cinema was now almost entirely realistic, cinematic realism was at first defined only by differentiating it

In 1928, Walt Disney (1901–1966) produced, *Steamboat Willie*, the first sound cartoon in the history of film. The hero, developed by Ub Iwerk for Disney the same year, is Mickey Mouse, who fights his way bravely through life and is tough enough, for the benefit of the audience, to put an end to the general crisis. Disney himself lent the figure, to whom he owes his leading position in cartoons, his own voice.

Disney led the pack in color film as well. As early as 1932, he paved the way, with *Flowers and Trees* from the "Silly Symphonies," for the three-color technicolor system.

from the escapist products of the "dream factory." Realistic film strives to concern itself with the real life of its viewer, not only to portray it but also to study it critically. Inspired by the new possibilities of the sound film, and under the influence of increasing social tensions, a group of filmmakers in the 1930s turned to realistic—social, societal, and contemporary—subject matter.

German film before 1933

In their silent films, the German directors of the New Objectivity had already moved the everyday life of minor employees and social outcasts into the limelight, especially Robert Siodmak's *People on Sunday* (1930), Murnau's *The Last Laugh* (1924), and Georg Wilhelm Pabst's *The Joyless Street* (1925). This socio-critical trend at the start of the 1930s took on political characteristics, as in Papst's anti-war film *West Front 1918* (1930), but also in Fritz Lang's detective film *M* (1931). Lang's film suggested a close association between the police and a criminal band, who together bring a child murderer to justice, and thus foreshadowed the political reality of Nazi terror. The politicization reached its peak in the proletariat

Fritz Lang skillfully inserted into his first sound film *M* (originally *Murderers among Us*) sounds, music, and voice for the expression of the subjective perceptions of the protagonist, played by Peter Lorre.

films promoted by the unions and worker parties of the Weimar Republic. *Kuhle Wampe or To Whom Does the World Belong?*, (1932), for which Bertolt Brecht wrote the script and Hanns Eisler the music, depicted the effects of mass unemployment through the example of a Berlin working family, and blamed

social democratic politics, among other factors, for the pervasive misery shown. Of course, with only 3.5 percent of the national production, socially and politically critical films made up only a small portion. They were, however, carefully watched, vigorously criticized, censored, and finally prohibited when the National Socialists took over. A large number of cinematic artists emigrated, including Fritz Lang, Max Ophüls, Reinhold Schnüzel, Robert Siodmak, Billy Wilder, Detlef Sierck (Douglas Sirk), Peter Lorre, Asta Nielsen and Elisabeth Bergner, to name only a few.

Josef von Sternberg's (1894–1969) *The Blue Angel* transformed the entirely unknown Marlene Dietrich (1901–1992) into an international star overnight in 1930. This film version of Heinrich Mann's social satire *Professor Unrat* is also famous for the skillful insertion of off-sounds. They supplemented the impressive picture composition, with its detailed and true-to-life sets, to create a hauntingly realistic atmosphere.

The poetry of reality

In France, the popular demand for French-language sound films in the 1930s led to the formation of smaller companies that were prepared to make it possible for young directors to work independently as artists. Out of such freedom resulted a series of realistic cinematic artworks which, in a way, are at the same time politically engaged and artistically creative. Films of various genres at this time could be grouped under the general heading "poetic realism:" melodramas, criminal films, adventure films, literary films, and social satires, all of which shared the characteristics of social engagement, detailed milieu description, and differentiated character description. Their fatalistic stories often revolved around figures at the fringes of society, who momentarily experienced happiness in love, but were ultimately left disappointed again.

In addition to the directors Jean Vigo, Marcel Pagnol, Julien Duvivier, and Marcel Carné, Jean

While the public accepted sound with enthusiasm, many artists—especially musicians who had become unemployed—warned against the "dangers of the sound film" in large-scale campaigns.

René Clair's early sound film *Under the Roofs of Paris* (1930) is an example of innovative use of sound that is appropriate to the medium. The dialogue is reduced to the most essential; sound and picture are brought into relationship with one another in such a way that they no longer parallel, but augment one another.

Daybreak (1939) told the story of a man who had murdered for love (Jean Gabin) as he waits through one night in his hotel room, surrounded by the police, the background of the crime revealed through a series of flashbacks. Marcel Carné (1909–1996) delivered a example typical of the style of "poetic realism" with its trademark mixture of stylization and naturalism, its melodrama and its social criticism.

Renoir (1894–1979) should be singled out. His films from these years influenced the international cinema as only productions from Hollywood ordinarily could. The son of the impressionist painter Auguste Renoir showed the world what realistic films were made of and explored all the cinematic possibilities that camera movement, use of natural lighting and original sound sources, and incorporation of landscape could offer. Most importantly, he discovered—even before Orson Welles—deep-focus photography. The use of lenses with great deep-focus capacity made it possible to depict elements at considerable distance from one another with equal sharpness, an effect known as depth of field. The vanishing point, toward which everything in the picture runs, creates relationships between all parts of the picture and also gives the smallest detail meaning. Using deep-focus photography with a movable camera, Renoir created a new cinematic language; instead of showing individual events in different scenes one after the other, he was able to join them to one another in an "inner montage." These long scenes, in which he was able to film complete plot segments without cutting, are called sequence shots. However, the excitement of Renoir's contemporaries over the cinematic innovations in his films of the 1930s was diminished by the generalized reaction to their content. Renoir's films made people uncomfortable because of their criticism of the times and their bitter skepticism, none of which the society of pre-war France wanted to hear. His masterpiece, *The Rules of the Game* (1939), was forbidden only a few weeks after its release for "demoralizing the people."

The British school of documentary film

In England, documentary filmmakers employed the new possibilities of realistic cinematic structuring.

This shot from *Toni* (1934) shows a typical example of Renoir's use of depth of focus. The sobering study was shot in a farm setting and anticipated the aesthetics of Italian neorealism, with its naturalistic pictures at original sites.

The director and producer John Grierson (1898–1972) gathered around him a group of young documentary filmmakers who wanted to bring their fellow citizens closer to the various cultures of the Empire, especially to the everyday lives of simple farmers, fishermen, miners, and industrial workers. Convinced of the educational possibilities of the documentary film for public edification and formation of opinion, he succeeded first in soliciting the help of state institutions and later from economic sponsors for his group's projects. The politically engaged filmmakers, however, did not satisfy themselves with portraying life in the Empire. In films such as *Housing Problems* (1935) or *Shipyard* (1937) they alluded to social problems. Out of consideration for their financial backers, however, they kept their criticism tame. Influenced by the Soviet revolu-

tionary film, the documentary filmmakers developed rhythmical montage techniques and borrowed

One of the most popular films by the British documentary filmmakers was *Night Mail* (1936). It shows the daily trip of a night train from London to Glasgow, underscored with music by Benjamin Britten and a poetic off-commentary by the poet W. H. Auden.

Enough to Eat? (1936) showed life in London's backyards during the 1930s.

filming methods from the feature film. They showed themselves to be especially creative in combined insertions of sounds, music, and spoken commentary.

The classical Hollywood movie

Some of the most noteworthy aesthetically innovative of the early sound films are indebted to the political and socially critical cinema of European heritage. The most successful ones worldwide came, however, from American producers. It was the great era of the classical Hollywood cinema; numerous new genres emerged, and Hollywood transformed itself into the "dream factory," whose suspenseful, happy, and extravagantly beautiful products allowed people a temporary flight from their bleak, everyday reality. Almost all genres propagated the myth of the country of unlimited possibilities and idealized, in endless variations, the "American dream" of a career that propelled one "from dishwasher to millionaire."

The epic *Gone with the Wind* (1939), the most expensive film produced up to that time, became the epitome of what was commonly viewed as great Hollywood cinema. It also surpassed, in that regard, the few films that had already been made with three-color technicolor. This tragedy of the unachievability of individual happiness in difficult times was the most-viewed cinema film of all time and garnered eight Oscars.

In new screen splendor... The most magnificent picture ever!

DAVID O. SELZNICK'S PRODUCTION OF MARGARET MITCHELL'S "GONE WITH THE WIND"

CLARK GABLE
VIVIEN LEIGH
LESLIE HOWARD OLIVIA de HAVILLAND

A SELZNICK INTERNATIONAL PICTURE · VICTOR FLEMING · SIDNEY HOWARD · METRO-GOLDWYN-MAYER INC.

Film as daydream: musicals

The sound film brought one particular genre to the forefront of film entertainment, one far removed from reality. After the enthusiastic reception of *The Jazz Singer*, it was natural to follow up by using the whole spectrum of sound art after the example of the thoroughly popular Broadway review, and to present it in "all-singing, all-dancing, all-talking films" on the screen. *Broadway Melody* (1929), the first film musical, tells within a sequence of review numbers a "backstage story," the fictional story of its making. From an advertising perspective, such effective mystification of show business

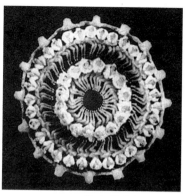

Busby Berkeley made the ensemble itself a protagonist; his dancers functioned as moving parts of a kaleidoscopic pattern in *42nd Street* (1933).

became a frequently chosen scenario in the new genre, which had struck like a bolt of lightning. In 1930, no fewer than 70 musicals were filmed in Hollywood. Busby Berkeley (1895–1976) choreographed some of the most expensive filmed review numbers of the 1930s for Warner Brothers. He seemed not only able to make his girls dance, but also his cameras, having them sway skillfully over ornate stage arrangements of scantily clad bodies on rotating floors or slide along from daring angles past hundreds of swinging, dancing legs. Meanwhile, RKO created a new type of romantic film musical around the dream pair Fred Astaire and Ginger Rogers, in which the opposing individual elements of dialogue, song, and dance were joined together in a unified plot typical of the later film musical. The simple love stories generally played out in the show business world, giving the heroes ample opportunity to express their feelings in emotional songs and elegant dances. Astaire's and Rogers' perfect harmony made it unmistakably clear that the characters they portrayed, despite initial irritations, were made for one another.

Fred Astaire and Ginger Rogers were the dream pair of American film musicals in the 1930s.

The flip side of the coin: gangster films

Musicals deflected the reality of the Depression by showing clearly what its viewers only dreamed, at the same time affirming that any crisis could be

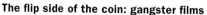

Little Caesar (1930), with Edward J. Robinson in the lead role, initiated the success of the gangster film.

overcome if a person would just sing energetically, dance, and be cheerful. But the nagging reality of the Depression was something even Hollywood could not keep at bay. On the contrary, the gangster film genre presented the myth of the "American dream" from the perspective that even members of the lower echelons of society could rise to power and money in this underworld variation.

The focus was the career of the "little guy," perhaps a soldier returning from the war or an unemployed youngster from the slums who eventually became the big gangster boss. Detectives played at best a secondary role in the gangster film. However, the point was not so much to understand crime as to show the exciting shadow economy of the prohibition era and the power struggles within the Mafia, whose real-life models fascinated the public. They were "films about newspaper headlines," as promised an advertising slogan of Warner Brothers, which specialized in this genre.

It was the sound film that first made it possible to make these stories about illegal casinos, dark warehouses, cheap hotel rooms, and poorly lit alleys so unsettlingly realistic. The classical gangster film is unimaginable without screeching brakes, rattling pistols, and the pithy slang typical of the underworld. The public sympathized openly with the brutal albeit humanly portrayed criminals, since the manufacturing and smuggling of alcohol merely satisfied a legitimate need in the eyes of most people.

This inevitably brought onto the scene women's organizations and churches, who stuck to their guns about criticizing the "glorification of crime" through the mostly infamous and violent ends of the gangster bosses portrayed. In 1929, the film industry

Both of the great gangster film stars of Warner Brothers, Humphrey Bogart and James Cagney, appeared together in *The Roaring Twenties* (1939). The film was later considered the apotheosis of the genre.

tried to counter possible censoring measures through the introduction of voluntary self control. They put together a list of eleven "Don'ts" and 25 "Be Carefuls," which most filmmakers more or less accepted while gritting their teeth. But closer examination of the matter reveals that it was less a matter of the protection of democracy or human rights than avoidance of taboos that could have led to public protests by conservative groups and, therefore, to income losses. The Motion Picture Production Code, as it was known, condemned not only cursing and French marriage beds, but also the portrayal of miscegenation and other alleged forms of sexual aberration. When the Production Code grew to include a list of crimes which were no longer allowed to be portrayed and advised against filming biographies of historical gangsters, there was a halt in production of the genre. The stars of the gangster films, James Cagney, Edward G.Robinson, and Humphrey Bogart, were for a time cast as detectives who, of course, often operated "undercover" and used methods similar to those of the criminals.

Along with gangster films, whose success was a result of the audiences' need to work through the dark reality of the Depression, there came about a series of directly socio-critical and pacifist films which propagated the political ideas of the New Deal. With *I Am a Fugitive from*

Scarface (1932), Howard Hawks' fictional biography of Al Capone, encountered difficulties with the censors. This gangster film contained more shooting, destruction, brutality, and murder than any of its predecessors.

Besides portrayal of violence, the new censorship groups tried to ban all forms of eroticism from the cinema. Mae West, whose famous erotic double entendres, such as "Come up and see me sometime," became household words, was one of the favorite targets of the Catholic "Legion of Decency" founded in 1934.

Citizen Kane (1941)

A high point of realistic filmmaking was Orson Welles' (1915–1985) complex character portrayal of a multi-millionaire. The rise and fall of Charles Foster Kane shows the shadowy side of the "American dream." How far, the film seemed to ask, have we come in a democracy which affords individual citizens, and especially the media, such power? The historical importance of Citizen Kane to the cinema is due, however, less to its story than to a number of striking innovations in the language of film. The English actor and director, who was perceived as a *Wunderkind*, hardly created anything new, but recombined all previously tried cinematic means of expression in an original way. Welles is indebted to his inventive camera man Gregg Toland for having revolutionized camera movement. The story is told in interlocking flashbacks from the point of view of several acquaintances of Kane. Welles underscored the subject unity of psychoanalytical recollection through rapid changes of perspective and extreme viewing angles. His use of the wide-angle lens with great depth of focus set new standards. He created meaning in his comprehensive sequence shots merely by placing the protagonist in the environment, and picture composition and movement in space replaced classical montage technique. Abundant special effects and innovative use of sound made the film one of the most admired of all time.

One of the most progressive American films of its time was John Ford's *The Grapes of Wrath* (1940), with the young Henry Fonda in a leading role. Through the example of an impoverished farming family during the Depression, the film mercilessly criticizes the effects of American capitalism and praised the reform work of Roosevelt's government.

a Chain Gang (1932), Mervyn LeRoy, for example, filmed a passionate appeal for the abolition of the inhumane system of penal colonies, and in *They Made Me a Criminal* (1939), Busby Berkeley emphatically called attention to factors that contribute to the commission of crimes for which society is responsible.

Horror films

Musicals and gangster films were not the only genres that first became popular with the sound film. Between 1930 and 1933, the horror film experienced a golden age that has yet to be surpassed today. Yet the genre was not new; the German expressionists had already discovered how much the public enjoyed allowing itself to be scared by stories about alien things that unexpectedly burst into an apparently safe and familiar world. The addition of sound could only heighten this effect. Creaking staircases, squeaking door hinges, howling owls and screeching women, the heartbeat of the victim, the cough of the approaching monster: All engendered images in the imagination of the audience, it was quickly recognized, that no mask or gloomy stage set could outdo. Vampires who avoided light, zombies, destructive maniacs, artificial people, and other creatures who populated the classical horror film only needed to be shown sparingly in the film after the introduction of sound. They remained in the shadows, as did their scientifically inexplicable origins. The horror film strikes at the primal fears of human beings in the face of the unknown and the super-powerful, conjuring up dangers that made the real needs of the audience seem comparatively harmless. The inevitable re-establishment of order at the end of the classical horror film points optimistically to a better future, which helps explain what experience has proven true: The horror film flourishes especially in bad times.

Immediately after *Dracula* (1930), which had caused hysteria among the public, Universal followed with *Frankenstein* (1931). Boris Karloff's (1887–1969) frightening and sensitive portrayal of the artificial man made him a star of the genre and established Universal as the leading producer of horror films.

Screwball comedy

The "screwball comedy" gave the cinema fan of the 1930s a more pleasant way to escape reality. This genre flourished between 1934 and 1945, and first emerged at the point when the world economic crisis had almost been conquered. From slapstick, the

The genre of the horror film intensified the development of new special effects. In order to avoid cuts and fade-outs in the transformation of *Dr. Jekyll and Mr. Hyde* (1931), the innovative director Rouben Mamoulian used a series of color filters one after the other, making different color mask layers visible.

Some of the most successful screwball comedies originated from the greatest director of the genre, Howard Hawks (1896–1977). The stars Katherine Hepburn and Cary Grant largely contributed to the success of *Bringing up Baby*.

The counterpart to the escapist screwball comedy was created by the irreverent Marx Brothers, with their anarchist comedies. In social satires such as *Animal Crackers* (1930), *Duck Soup* (1933) or *A Night at the Opera* (1935), the main point was always the intentional undermining of the dignity of the middle-class world and its sacred cows such as art, military heroism, or the opera.

comedy form of the silent film era, it adopted the quick pace and frequent visual gags. Rapid-fire dialog duels gush forth and are the main source of its comedy. The eccentric characters of the screwball comedy could hardly let their partners have their say; they outdid one another with their wit and snappy comebacks. Typically the stories are far removed from reality, taking place in mileaus frequented by rich people working hard to enjoy themselves, yet here too, as in the horror film, the focus is also on the re-establishment of order. Conflicts arise from, for example, reversed gender roles. Either unconventional, unruly women or shy and withdrawn men are "tamed," after all sorts of confusions, on the parts of their more rational partners.

Propaganda and entertainment in Nazi cinema

In Germany, the National Socialists had isolated all opposing groups and parties immediately after they assumed power in 1933, gradually bringing under their control all the organizations that had roles in the formation of public opinion in order to bring them into their new propaganda system. The propaganda minister Joseph Goebbels personally took charge of the cinema, and his effectiveness was especially highly regarded. An enthusiastic fan of the cinema himself, he knew the public's preferences well enough to know that one could bring political ideas to the people under the guise of apparently

"This won't bring the world to an end," Zarah Leander comforted her public in *Die Grosse Liebe* (1942), a typical German "stay-the-course" film. Entertainment alone is the best propaganda, Goebbels believed, and most of the films put out during the Nazi regime therefore offered suspenseful, cheerful, or sentimental entertainment. With the exception of direct propaganda, these films lobbied implicitly for the Nazi ideology of supermen and born leaders or offered optimistic models for privately surviving the war.

harmless entertainment films. The typical National Socialist film offered suspense, fun, or a tragic lesson and integrated skillful propagandizing toward the goals of the National Socialists. Popular stars such as Hans Albers, Zarah Leander, Marika Rökk and Heinz Rühmann were effective in propagating new governing structures and values such as obedience and acceptance of fate in their films, encouraging the mobilization for the conquest of the world, and exhibiting boundless optimism. The use of blatant propaganda films turned out to be relatively minor. Only in preparation for "extraordinary measures" were specific smear campaigns launched against the "enemies of the Reich." In 1940, for example, Veit Harlan's anti-Semitic work *Jud Süss* appeared—shortly after the first time Hitler had taken a public position on the "final solution of the Jewish question." Otherwise, National Socialist propaganda presented itself this bluntly only in the documentary films and weekly news reels. The films of Leni Riefenstahl (b.1902), *Triumph of the Will* (1935) about the party convention of 1934 and *Olympia* (1938) about the Olympic

The pseudo-documentary film *The Eternal Jew* (1940) exceeded even *Jud Süss* in its smear tactics. Both films were shown to systematically prepare mostly soldiers, the SS, the police, and the populations of the districts where the concentration camps for genocide were located.

"The logical result of Fascism is the introduction of aesthetics into political life. The violation of the masses, whom Fascism, with its Fuehrer cult, forces to their knees, has its counterpart in the violation of the apparatus which is pressed into the production of ritual values. All efforts to render politics aesthetic culminate in one thing: war."
Walter Benjamin, The Work of Art in the Age of Mechanical Reproduction, *1936*

The glorification of the athletic body in Leni Riefenstahl's *Olympia* (1938).

Games of 1936, are discussed today as much as examples of the high art of the documentary film as of fascist aesthetics. Close attention to picture composition and its skillful connection to rhythmical montage, defended later by the director as non-political means of expression, are in Riefenstahl's work entirely in the service of the Führer cult and the glorification of National Socialist ideology.

Anti-Hitler films

Up until its entry into the war, Washington carried out an isolationist policy and attempted to take a neutral position with regard to Nazi Germany. In Hollywood, where many European immigrants had long been willingly and thankfully accepted, an interventionist counter-movement formed in the mean time. As more and more became known about the brutal annexation policies

Chaplin pulled out all the stops in his art as director, main actor, and composer of *The Great Dictator*. He even brought the beloved little tramp back to life in his first sound film; the Jewish barbarian released from the concentration camp is mistaken for the dictator, a caricature of Hitler, and finds an opportunity for a passionate speech on the behalf of humanity, peace, and justice.

and the political terror wreaked by the National Socialist regime within Germany, artists became increasingly politically involved against fascism. Charlie Chaplin's satire *The Great Dictator* (1938–1940) was one of the first Hollywood films that attempted to convince the American public of the necessity of a strengthened American engagement in Europe. In 1939, Anatole Litvak warned in *Confessions of a Nazi Spy* (1939) of the infiltration of the United States by National Socialist thinking. In *Man Hunt* (1941), Fritz Lang told the story of a British parachutist who jumps out over Germany in order to shoot Hitler. With *Foreign Correspondent* (1940), *Saboteur* (1942), and *Lifeboat* (1943) even Alfred Hitchcock, who otherwise refrained from any sort of political engagement, contributed to anti-Nazi propaganda.

When Hitler's conquest of Western Europe caused economic losses felt by the American film industry—in 1940, U.S. films could only be exported to neutral states such as Sweden, Portugal, or Switzerland—Hollywood also integrated the war theme into its typical entertainment films. The extraordinary war situation offered a setting that was well-suited to heightening tension in countless thrillers and melodramas. The most famous example to combine patriotic message and the box-office appeal of a star-studded melodrama is Michael Curtiz's *Casablanca* (1942).

The hero, Rick, at first takes a very privately isolationist position, but finally turns from the woman he loves in favor of the resistance fighter Victor. The film propagates the renunciation of individual happiness in the face of more pressing social demands, but simultaneously gives sustenance to the dream of a very great love between a man and a woman.

Casablanca became a cult film in the 1960s and 1970s. The story took place in "a world unhinged" and described society's outsiders, with whom the youthful intellectuals of these years could identify.

Even Walt Disney made his contribution to anti-fascist propaganda during the Second World War.

If the government had reproached Hollywood before the entry into the war for "inciting the public," from 1942 on the strike forces themselves contributed to the establishment of the Chaplin-promoted "second front" by commissioning propaganda films, such as the weekly series *Why We Fight* (1942–1945). A scene from *The Battle of Britain* (1943).

Today, films are available in many different formats. For a long time, the film industry fought television and upbraided it as a threat to the movies and the art of film. Yet, among other things, we owe our broad familiarity with movie history and films from many foreign countries and, especially, high quality films to television where they first appeared rather than in the movie theaters. Television today has begun to function as a journalistic, educational, and entertaining medium,

During the 1950s, television, with its brief, daily programming, still delivered events that the new viewers did not want to miss for any reason.

roles previously reserved for other media, whereby the impact of these other media has been formative, not destructive. Television reaches more people than any other form of communication, therefore lending itself to reaching the many particular interests of the public. Producers of goods and opinion makers of all types have made television into the most attractive of all advertising domains. Its critics, however,

consider it asocial, damaging to the imagination, and dangerous to youth, criticisms which in their day were also leveled at the theater, the novel, and, in our century, also about the cinema, which today already enjoys a higher degree of respect than does television.

Yet television is a phenomenon not much newer than cinematography. Attempts to develop television at the same time as the telephone can be traced back into the 19th century. Television technology involves transforming the light value of pictures line for line (first divided into 60, and today into 625 lines) into electronic signals and sending them to a receiver that transforms them back again into pictures. German television pioneer Paul Nipkow devised the first usable mechanical image analyzer, the perforated, rotating Nipkow plate, at the same time the Lumières were working on their cinematograph. It took more than 30 years, until 1928 in America and 1929 in England and Germany, for the first test pictures and experimental broadcasts to be conducted.

The most important steps toward modern, fully electronic television technology were the developments of electronic picture scanners by the American Vladimir Zvorykin and the German physicist Manfred von Ardenne. The first regular broadcasts already took place in the 1930s; however, the future mass medium lacked the necessary infrastructure—

hardly anyone owned a receiver or even wanted one. The National Socialists, who had recognized the potential of the new medium early on and made a concerted effort to promote its testing, set up the first public television rooms in Berlin, in which the populace was able to watch the first large-scale television broadcast on the occasion of the 1939 Olympic games. The Germans were to become a nation of television viewers. In the same year in America the radio network NBC, which already possessed a fully electronic technology, started its television programming, but even in the otherwise advanced United States, at that time there were no more than 200 television sets ready to receive transmissions. The first regular broadcasts both here and abroad dealt with political events; from 1944 on, boxing and wrestling matches were broadcast in the United States.

Only after the war, which caused the spread of television to stagnate because all the electronic firms were retooling for war production, was the time ripe for television. Once again, the Americans took the lead: in 1947 they began mass-producing TV receivers, and by 1948 a million households were watching television. Television spread explosively during the following years. In 1952 there were 15 million television sets in United States, in 1953 24 million, and today over 90 percent of all households have at least one television.

Along with the American cinema, TV offerings from the United States also became successful export articles. The Cartwright men from the Ponderosa Ranch on "Bonanza" made television history in Germany.

While television in the United States was organized from the start by private enterprise, the BBC represents the model for a predominantly publicly owned television system in Europe. In West Germany, after the experience of the Nazi regime having taken control of all media, there was a move to prevent state influence on programming. The concept developed by the Western occupation forces for a cooperative of broadcast institutions in Germany, the ARD, provided for governing boards composed of representatives from all relevant social groups to oversee the broadcasters while ownership transferred to the public control of the states. The broadcasters of the ARD, as well as of the Second German Television (ZDF) established in 1963, are financed up to today from fees and advertising, whereby the broadcast time for commercial advertising is limited to twenty minutes a day and must be broadcast before 10 p.m.

"The Wheel of Fortune," is a mixture of game show and advertising. The concept has been exported to a total of 27 countries throughout the world, so that a hundred million people follow the simple game weekly. Sponsors hope that the viewers will potentially purchase one of the prizes awarded.

As early as 1954 the Americans were in the position of broadcasting in color; in West Germany, Chancellor Willi Brandt gave the go-ahead in 1967 for the American PAL system, while the state operated television of East Germany and the Soviet Union adopted the French SECAM.

The programming in West Germany emphasized education and information and its offerings accordingly included live television plays adapted from challenging theatrical plays and serious news magazines. But in the United States the three great networks, NBC, CBS, and ABC, competed from the start not only for a viewing public but also for advertisers, who established the trends in content. The most popular fare in America has long been entertainment and game shows, soap operas, and detective series, sport, quiz shows, and infotainment—all formats which today determine TV programming throughout the world and have become specific to the medium of television.

In the United States around 1970 a new media market established itself with satellite, cable, and pay TV, in which one decodes a scrambled program with a rented decoder; a growing number of channels and programs began to compete. By the beginning of the 1990s, the new broadcast technology, and private television with it, established themselves in Europe. Already in Italy in 1974, commercial providers of programs were permitted to broadcast; France and Germany followed between 1981 and 1987, while Belgium, Spain, and Portugal introduced the dual system with publicly owned and private broadcasters in 1987.

The expansion of the group of providers has, with the multitude of channels, brought about an innovation: the television nation no longer views the same programs, and increasingly fewer people can discuss in the morning a certain evening program they saw in common. The increase in the available channels le an enormous demand for new programs.

Originally highly nationality-specific, television of European countries has been importing an increasing number of American products since the 1970s. The rating leaders of the great networks, *Dynasty*, *Dallas*, and *Columbo*, as well as American-style game shows, talk shows, and late night shows also achieved enormous popularity in Germany, bringing in the highest ratings. The family series, a typical American product, developed as an invocation of a perfect world in the 1950s and 1960s into a more and more realistic appraisal of family relationships. While the loathsome family member tyrannizes the entire family in *Dallas* and *Dynasty*, the most popular series of the 1990s, *Married With Children* and *The Simpsons*, sarcastically show all family members as greedy and self-interested hedonists, who are only interested in consumer goods and television.

While the public attending the present-day cinema is looking for fairy tales, adventure, and spectacle, it demands from TV an especially genuine semblance of reality. How else is the great success of the new genre "reality TV" to be explained, which joins reporting with catastrophe voyeurism? Real accidents and crimes are re-enacted for these broadcasts at the original sites of the events. The biggest world-wide television event to date with the highest ratings

since the inception of television was the 1997 funeral of Princess Diana, on whose comings and goings the media consumers from all over the world had fed almost without pause.

The future of television could potentially intertwine the fiction of manipulated images with the reality of viewers to an even greater degree. In the foreseeable future, interactive television could provide the individual viewer access to the central computer of a media provider. The user may then, in a video-on-demand program, not only choose between different films but even decide on preferred plots, determine the camera angle during live sporting events, and place orders for goods directly after commercials. It remains to be seen which media format will eventually establish itself—pay TV, privately financed television, or sponsored broadcasts. Or perhaps the public of the future, tired of commercials and zapping, will bring about a renaissance of the publicly owned system.

Private broadcasters finance themselves exclusively by selling advertising time. In contrast to publicly owned broadcasters, who can advertise around the clock.

The new world order after the war

Europe, freed in 1945 from National Socialism, lay in ruins and ashes. Countless people had died on the battlefields and beneath the hail of bombs or had been murdered by the horrible, state-sponsored death machinery of the Nazis. Industry and homes had been destroyed, and a stream of returning soldiers and refugees moved through the ravaged landscape trying to gain a foothold on a new life. News of the true extent of the Nazi terror graphically showed how quickly even democratic societies of the Christian-humanistic tradition could be perverted by cynical systems of injustice, in which economics, politics, and population are equally prepared to take part in repression and organized genocide, or at least not to resist it. Together with the difficulty of meeting the most basic physical needs during the years immediately following the war, this recognition led to deep insecurity in the survivors. They were filled with a strong desire for material security and reliable values.

For a short time, pacifist, radical democratic, and socialist ideas experienced popularity in Western Europe. The reconstruction of European industry, supported heavily by the Marshall Plan of the United States, led (especially in Germany) to an "economic

In the period directly after the war, films that dealt with events of the recent past, war, fascism and post-war misery were the exception. Wolfgang Staudte's *Murderers Among Us* (1946) was one of the few German films that made a serious attempt to grapple with issues of collective guilt for wartime atrocities.

miracle," which established a consumer mentality and unconditional belief in progress as central values of the new Western society. While the United States gained loyal allies in Western Europe, the Soviet Union held Eastern Europe firmly in its grasp. In the competition of the two new superpowers for dominance in world politics, the fronts were quickly defined and hardened rapidly into the restorative politics of the Cold War. Fear of an uncertain future crippled the desire to come to terms with the past, leading Germany to re-militarization, and the developed nations of the world into an absurd and costly nuclear arms race.

Film at the zero hour: Italian neorealism

Shortly after the liberation of Italy by the Allied forces, Roberto Rossellini (1906–1977) completed a film in 1945 that he had been secretly preparing during the period of occupation, initiating one of the most fruitful and influential artistic movements in the history of Italian cinema. *Open City* (1945) made connections between the fates of its characters, anti-fascist resistance fighters from different ideological camps, and conveyed an extraordinarily authentic picture of the desperate atmosphere of the last years of the war, despite the plot's tendency towards melodrama.

Rossellini's realism was merciless: All the main characters in the film, the Communist resistance fighters, the loving woman who hides them, and the anti-fascist Catholic priest, are shockingly and almost casually wiped out during the course of the film, some even before the eyes of a paralyzed population. The director may have appalled his public with the film's brutal portrayal of terror, but he did so in order to point out the responsibility of the individual for fascist terror, and to set in motion a critical evaluation of the recent past. *Open City* marked not only the first foray into a new subject matter, but also a conscious break with formal traditions, particularly

Following the war, the public was more interested in repressing instead of overcoming wartime horrors, leading to the success of purposefully timeless films that upheld old, familiar values: Marcel Carné's *Children of Paradise* (1945).

As early as 1942, the Italian film *Ossessione* (Ital. "Obsession") heralded a shift away from fascist aesthetics toward realism. Though the film was heavily cut by censors, Luchino Visconti (1906–1976) and other young directors began a theoretical discussion in the magazine *Cinema* that paved the way for neorealism.

93

the polished aesthetics of the optimistic entertainment cinema of the fascist era.

Rossellini had made something positive out of the fact that the film studios were in crisis, with the accompanying lack of refined techniques, raw film, and professional actors. In just a few takes he filmed scenes at original locations with non-professional actors, among whom he mixed only a few professionals including the later stars Anna Magnani and Aldo Fabrizi, creating a semblance of reality previously unachievable in fictional film.

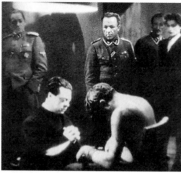

Open City was the most-often viewed film in Italy in 1945 and one of the few neorealistic films that became a worldwide success. Federico Fellini received an Oscar for the script.

Instead of leading his viewers to psychologically and subjectively identify with his characters, he aimed to create for them an intellectual distance from which they could survey various cause-and-effect relationships. He intentionally left out the typical elements that tied plots neatly together in order to avoid a classical buildup of tension according to the American model. The tragic episodes of the film therefore stand next to each other as if by chance, lending the film the character of an unbiased chronicle.

The contrast between these and the other type of films being made in Italy at the time, the so-called "*telefoni-bianchi*" or "white telephone" films, which were supposed to divert attention from social reality with their glamorous studio sets and superficial plots set in upper-class environments, could not have been more stark. After the first success of Italian post-war cinema,

Paisan relates the freeing of Italy by the Allied troops in six episodes. Rossellini worked spontaneously, without a script, and let himself be inspired by the reality of the shooting locations.

Bicycle Thieves is a quintessential example of neorealistic cinema, and without doubt belongs to the canon of classic films.

Rossellini dedicated himself to dealing with war and fascism in two further neorealistic episodic films, *Paisan* (1946) and *Germany: Year Zero* (1947).

"Every person is a hero" (Cesare Zavattini)

Other young directors turned to the second great theme of neorealism, the everyday life of common people in post-war Italy. Vittorio de Sica's (1902–1974) *Bicycle Thieves* (1948) tells the story of the unemployed Antonio Ricci, whose bicycle is stolen on his first day working at his urgently needed new job mounting placards, leaving him without the means of transportation that was a condition of his employment. Desperate not to become unemployed yet again, he pursues the thief back and forth through Rome, and in the end himself turns to thievery and steals a bicycle.

The actor and director Vittorio de Sica (1901–1974), together with his script writer Cesare Zavattini, directed several of the most important films of neorealism: *Shoeshine* (1946), *Bicycle Thieves* (1948), *Miracle in Milan* (1950) and *Umberto D* (1951).

Like Rossellini, de Sica used exclusively original settings and non-professional actors. Instead of showing people the great conflicts of the historical period, he concentrated on the commonplace, the everyday cares of people—on the objectification of individual fate. The scenes were not arranged according to linear causality, but chronologically.

Life, which in reality was experienced as disconnected and fragmented, was also to be portrayed in cinema in its inscrutability and

One of the few commercial successes among neorealistic films was Giuseppe de Santis' *Bitter Rice* (1949). Its box-office draw had less to do with its socio-critical portrayal of the exploitation of Piedmont rice workers than the erotic magnetism of the lead actress, Silvana Mangano.

randomness. De Sica's scriptwriter, Cesare Zavattini formulated the theoretical basis of the neorealistic movement as a clear rejection of classical, contrived Hollywood staging, which superimposed an artificial pattern over the multiplicity of complex social reality. Driven by a need for abstract relationships, neorealism transferred the focus to "real things, as they are." The films were not supposed to narrate but to portray, and, since there were no suspenseful plot climaxes to be emphasized, the storyline could not be neatly wrapped up; endings had to be left as open as any person's life is.

Zavattini's theoretical article "Some Ideas on the Cinema" (published 1953) suggested the formation of a movement. However, it never really gained enough momentum to became a "school" and soon disintegrated, after the innovative outburst of the immediate post-war years, into the disparate signatures of its creators, who directed their attention with renewed enthusiasm to folkloristic, everyday human or Christian themes.

Neorealism's relatively rapid demise was prompted by massive criticism from all directions. The Church took offense at the anti-clerical tone and the unrestrained treatment of sexuality in the films, official government circles objected to their crass but realistic portrayal of social iniquities that they would rather have smoothed over, while the political left complained about the pessimistic

"Neorealism has this as its goal: To give all people the courage, to give them the consciousness, to the human beings. The term neorealism implies—in the broadest sense—rejection of the technical-professional work staff, the script writer included. Handbooks, programs, grammars no longer have any meaning. Even designations such as close-up, reverse shot, etc. no longer have any meaning. Each person has his own personal film script. Neorealism breaks through all patterns, rejects all rules, which are basically nothing more than codification of restrictions. It is reality which breaks these patterns. For there are endless possibilities of encountering reality for a man of the cinema (one only needs to walk with the camera through a setting). There can be, *a priori*, no close-ups."

Cesare Zavattini, "Some Ideas on the Cinema," 1953

titude and absence of a definite political stance. he so-called "Andreotti Law," which had just een passed in Italy, connected financial support or film ventures to a series of censorship measures, with the predictable result that only accommodating ox-office successes would be supported by state ubsidies. At the same time, Hollywood once again ooded the Italian market with products that met he needs of people who wanted nothing more han to forget their wartime suffering far better han did the critical self-examination nd moral renewal called for by the eorealistic films.

By the beginning of the 1950s, eorealism's former proponents ad already turned their attention o more successful and economic- lly profitable forms of film. However, the influence of Italian eorealism on the world cinema was far greater than its immediate ffectiveness and spread far. Its ypical stylistic characteristics were further eveloped by upcoming young directors through- ut the world, and became a modern-day form of inema.

Billy Wilder's *The Lost Weekend* (1945) is one of the few *film noir* movies that do not have crime as a theme. It was also the first film to deal with alcoholism in a manner that was, while shocking, also serious and unromantic.

HUMPHREY **BOGART** · MARY **ASTOR**

the **Maltese Falcon**

"Never get involved with a client," advised private detective Sam Spade in *The Maltese Falcon* (directed by John Huston, 1941), the first Bogart movie to become a cult film.

Film noir

The shadows cast by the Second World War made their way even into Hollywood's film production. French critics coined the term *film noir* in 1946 for a style which manifested itself in various Hollywood genres—the melodrama, Western, musical, and especially the criminal film. The films of the "black series," as it was called in Germany, dealt mostly with murder and crime but, in contrast to the gangster films of the 1930s, which are without a doubt the precursors of *film noir*, the borders between good and evil became cloudy. The mayor, for example, would be head of the crime syndicate, and the hero would have to kill in order not to be killed himself.

With ice cold calculation and murderish charm Barbara Stanwyck played the title role in Billy Wilder's melodrama *Double Indemnity* (1944) and established her reputation as the coldest *femme fatale* in *film noir*.

The first films of this type emerged at the beginning of the 1940s, and reflected the mood of hopeless resignation and disillusionment which dampened American optimism during the war. For the first time, American society fully experienced the stress and deprivations of a total, global war. The criminal case in *film noir* became at the same time a backdrop for a pessimistic commentary on society: War raged not only in distant Europe but also on the streets of American big cities, and, above all, in relationships between men and women.

For *film noir* directors, the atmosphere in their films was more important than the plausibility of their plots. During the shooting of *The Big Sleep* (directed by Howard Hawks, 1945) there was supposedly great confusion about who the chauffeur's murderer actually was, which even the author, Raymond Chandler, could not clarify.

From "good bad girls" to *femmes fatales*

The societal restructuring caused by the war resulted in great insecurity and role conflicts between the sexes. While the vast majority of men had been off at war, women had stepped into roles and taken over social responsibilities traditionally reserved for men in times of peace, not only in the family but also at the workplace. Like its literary predecesors, writers of criminal stories such as Raymond Chandler, Dashiel Hammett and James M. Cain, *film noir* chiefly addressed a male public. The films' broken male protagonists were typically confronted with women who were in equal measure both beautiful and self-assured. These fascinating women exerted a strong erotic attraction on the heroes. Until the endings, however, it remained unclear whether behind the intimidating, "bad" (i. e., nontraditional) characteristics lay hidden a good girl, the "good bad girl," or a *femme fatale* who would endanger the hero and cast herself into ruin.

Gusts of wind, candle-light, and macabre shadows complement the motif of the winding stairs which lead into chaos in the criminal thriller *The Spiral Staircase* (1945) by Robert Siodmak.

Typical stylistic characteristics

John Huston's (1906–1987) directing debut, *The Maltese Falcon* (1941), was the first film to reveal the stylistic characteristics which were to establish themselves as esthetic conventions of the *film noir*. The hard-boiled private detective Sam Spade, sometimes in competition with, and sometimes together with a group of gangsters, tracks down a mysterious statuette. While the work of art proves to be a forgery in the end, Spade discovers that his attractive female client, with whom he has perhaps fallen in love, is a murderer.

Rita Hayworth, first celebrated in Hollywood as the ideal of the feminine American, was disenchanted forever in the famous mirror scene from *The Lady from Shanghai* (directed by Orson Welles, 1946), and became instead the quintessential dangerous *femme fatale*.

Nothing appeared reliable and consistent in this inscrutable plot, and the uncertainty of the characters found meaningful expression in the sinister illumination. Darkness, side lighting, and foot lighting dominated in the harsh black white contrasts of the pictures, and even daylight scenes were illuminated as if they were night scenes. Counter light shots, bordering shadows, and shots from unusual camera angles left the detective, who is searching for explanations, as much in the dark as the audience. This typical use of light—for example, the staircase scenes and mirror shots that became popular in the later *film noir*—calls to mind German *Caligarism* of the 1920s. Actually, a group of German directors who emigrated to Holly-wood contributed enormously to the *film noir*, among them Billy Wilder, Fritz Lang, Anatole Litvak, Robert Siodmak and Fred Zinnemann.

Only one important character-istic of the *film noir* was absent from *The Maltese Falcon*: Many later films allowed the audience to experience the events taking place through the subjective perspective of the hero, whose voice tells the story in flashbacks from off-camera. Through the interlocking of the time frames, heroes of the *film noir* films were cut off from their future again and again. The past, according to the message of this dark, fatalistic narrative style, would continue to weigh on them eternally; progress hardly seemed possible.

The *film noir* style was not limited to Hollywood. The British Carol Reed shot the dismal criminal story *The Third Man* (1949), with Orson Welles in the lead role, in the rubble of war-damaged Vienna, making effective use of con-trast and shadows, and lots of tilted camera angles. The film score of the zither player Anton Karas became world famous.

The world comes undone

After the end of the war, the genre of *film noir* expanded further. Instead of the romantic figure of the lone private detective, soldiers returning from the war moved onto center stage, disoriented from the horrors they had experienced and alienated from their once familiar surroundings, seeking to re-establish their places in society. Films were now made outside the studios, as well, in nighttime urban settings, on rain-soaked streets, and between warehouses and bars. In the 1950s, the ambivalent heroes of the *film noir* seemed to doubt society. They become entangled deeper and deeper in crime which, even in the earliest *film noir*, blurred the distinction between victims and perpetrators. Even the aesthetic structure of these films lent support to this impression of a world gone mad.

A late masterpiece of the *film noir* is Orson Welles' *Touch of Evil* (1957). A corrupt sheriff, who cannot come to terms with the death of his wife, falsifies proof with an egomania ranging from obsessive to downright sinister in order to solve criminal cases more quickly. Extreme perspectives and angular shots like Welles had already used in *Citizen Kane*, sharp light/dark contrasts and long shadows accentuated the growing insanity of the anti-hero, creating an oppressive and ominous atmosphere. The film shows a world ruled by the Mafia, drug smuggling, and murder, in which the guardians of the law also participate.

As in Germany, where a critical confrontation with the horrifying events of the recent past was the exception in the so-called *Trümmerfilme* (rubble films) popular at the time, and in Italy, where neo-realism did not seem to sit comfortably with the young, upcoming republic's view of itself, the trend of the *film noir* in America soon gave way once again, by popular demand, to the superficial cinema of entertainment.

Gary Cooper belonged to the first group of Hollywood greats, including Jack L. Warner, Ronald Reagan, Louis B. Mayer, Adolphe Menjou, Robert Taylor, and Walt Disney, who, as "friendly witnesses," willingly informed the public about the supposed Communist infiltration of Hollywood.

Along with Humphrey Bogart and Lauren Bacall, who led a march to protest the HUAC hearings, other stars including Danny Kaye, John Huston, William Wyler, Jane Wyatt, and June Havoc publicly expressed their outrage about the Communist-hunt.

Witch hunt and restoration

With the arrival of the Cold War, the socio-cultural climate of the United States changed. After fascism had been conquered, people concentrated on a new threat that united the nation—the perceived Communist danger. The beginnings of anti-Communist campaigns occurred during Truman's time in office. Trials

against the leaders of the American Communist Party and suspicious "New Deal" intellectuals, which were supposed to "stem" the Communist threat, introduced the shameful phase of "McCarthyism," in which Senator Joseph McCarthy, the feared Communist hunter, unleashed a veritable witch hunt against diverse influential personalities of public life.

Even Hollywood came under enormous pressure through the activities of McCarthy's committee

against "un-American activities" (HUAC). It counted on the fact that the questioning of film stars would make headlines and at the same time could ensure that the film industry, which was eager to conform, would offer only minimal resistance to its "cleansing methods."

One of the few socio-critical Hollywood productions of the post-war period, which addressed themes such as unemployment, corruption in the armed forces and racism, is William Wyler's *The Best Years of Our Lives* (1946), which illuminated the issues raised by soldiers returning home from the front at all levels of society.

This soon revealed itself to be an accurate prediction. In 1947, the first 10 "unfriendly witnesses," the "Hollywood 10," were put in jail for up to a year and then blacklisted because of their refusal to testify in front of the committee, which led to their inability to work; afterward, the "friendly witnesses" concerned themselves with forcefully underscoring their anti-Communist thinking in the hearings. In the process there were abstruse confessions, like that of Robert Taylor, who stated in testimony that Hollywood should remain apolitical and make anti-Communist films. Walt Disney's testimony that his Mickey Mouse character was threatened by world Communism since there had been workers' strikes at his studio, seemed similarly paranoid.

More important than the testimonies themselves was the appearance of stars before the committee, which publicly legitimated its activity. A spontaneously called protest, which pointed to the fact that the hearings conflicted with the guaranteed rights and freedoms of the American Constitution, led to the interrogations being postponed for four years. However, when the committee resumed its work in 1951, many film artists, including Elia Kazan, Edward G. Robinson and Sterling Hayden, saved their careers from damage by denouncing others. Anyone who was called to testify and did not was automatically labeled as guilty, added to the growing list of the "blackballed," and had to deal with the fact that they would no longer be employed.

German *Heimat* films (sentimental films with national themes) were often remakes of films from the 1930s, as was the greatest public success of the decade: *Grün ist die Heide* ("The Green Moors," 1951) by Hans Deppe. Like many of his colleagues, Deppe, who was already quite productive during the Third Reich, could continue his career uninterrupted after the war. It is no wonder that the rebuilt German film industry showed little interest in a critical examination of the past.

The effects of the witch hunt on the film industry were devastating. Only 10 percent of the artists who were blacklisted were later able to re-establish their careers. Almost panic-stricken, the film producers suppressed all critical overtones, so that the film of the 1950s, after a short blossoming of socio-critical and realistic films, returned to what was safe and remained uniform and superficial.

The film offerings met the need of the world's public caught up in the economic upswing, to suppress and divert unpleasantness. The flood of glamorous musicals, sentimental melodramas, and costly historical spectacles coming from Hollywood corresponded to the boom in Germany of *Heimat*

Extraterrestrial invasions characteristically threatened to come from the "red planet," named after the Roman god of war, Mars. So it was in *Red Planet Mars* (1952), *The War of the Worlds* (1953), *Invaders from Mars* (1953) and *Devil Girl From Mars* (1954).

Shaken and made suspicious by the Cold War, Americans feared aggressive invasions as well as a more subtle infiltration of Communism. This fear found expression in *Invasion of the Body Snatchers* (1956), for example, in which the threat takes place within the people themselves: the extra-terrestrials clone the residents of a small town and replace the people with their emotionless doubles.

films, which conjured up an unproblematic world with established norms, a dream which even National Socialism and war apparently had not shaken. A further indicator of the restorative mood of the postwar period was the fact that in hardly any other phase of international film history were so many remakes of familiar, previously successful films produced as there were between 1949 and 1955.

Cinematic banning of the "red menace"

The fear widespread among Americans about the infiltration of society by communism or even by an invasion of Communist troops was not only fed by the activities of McCarthy's committee, but also by Hollywood. At the beginning of the 1950s, a wave of science fiction films, a genre that had previously received little attention, grew and suddenly became the most prolific genre. The imagined fear, in countless variations, of an invasion of extraterrestrials proved to be ripe for projection of the underlying fears of the "red menace" which could, through translation into a fictional future, not only be expressed but also faced.

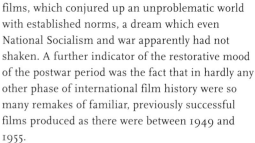

Hollywood lent support to the call for nuclear armament by portraying it as the preferred means of defense. The aliens were portrayed as bloodcurdling monsters, as in *The Thing from Another World* (1951), or as relentless combatants similar to those in *The War of the Worlds* (1953), who react to offers of peace and communication with aggression. With creatures of such gross inhumanity, the films clearly indicated, the use of nuclear defense measures like the atom bomb are not only legitimate but necessary.

A firm critical of the invasion paranoia and arms race mentality was *The Day the Earth Stood Still* (1951).

At the same time, a contrasting series of science fiction films focused on people's fear of atomic war and its consequences, the inevitable consequences

A picture from prosperous years: in 1943 movie theaters stayed open into the wee hours of the morning for factory workers coming after the late shift.

stemming from the fruits of a scientific community no longer governed by ethical concerns. In *The Day the Earth Stood Still* (1951), an emissary from a distant planet warns humankind of the dangers of nuclear war and commands them to maintain peace. Jack Arnold (1916–1992), the master of the genre, created *The Incredible Shrinking Man* (1957) who, due to the effects of a nuclear fog, shrinks to the size of a match and has to live in a dollhouse. In his classic *Tarantula* (1955), by way of contrast, he has a spider grow out of control; but again, it is naive researchers whose unchecked curiosity brings humanity into danger.

The end of the studio system

Observed today, the film productions typical of the 1950s, especially those of Hollywood, give one the impression of a film world that is ever richer, more colorful, more elaborate, and more glamorous. Actually, the film industry experienced one of its most serious crises in the 1950s, which it was only able to survive by undergoing dramatic structural changes. As late as 1946, box office receipts continued to exceed all previous records, and accounting for inflation, that year was perhaps economically the most successful ever for the film industry. The whole world was going to the movies; in the United States alone, where over 500 films were produced during that year, 50 percent of the

Preston Sturges (1898–1959) had already made a name for himself as a particularly witty script writer before he fascinated his public in the 1940s with a fine feel for comic timing, the witty dialogue of his eccentric figures, and brilliant visual gags in his black and satirical comedies. His greatest success was *The Lady Eve* (1941), with Henry Fonda and Barbara Stanwyck in the lead roles.

MR. STURGES

The Dane Detlef Sierck (1900–1987) continued his career, begun in Germany, in Hollywood as Douglas Sirk. He owes his renown to a successful series of elaborately produced melodramas including *Magnificent Obsession* (1953), *Written on the Wind* (1957) and *Imitation of Life* (1958). With virtuousity he pulled all the stops; using expressive coloration, innovative images, and emotion-heightening dramatic music, he brought tears to one's eyes while offering pointed social criticism.

Billy Wilder (*1906), who has produced most of his own films since 1951, distinguished himself in the 50s with a cynical view of the film industry in *Sunset Boulevard* (1950), biting erotic comedies like *The Seven Year Itch* (1955) and *Some Like it Hot* (1959), as well as ironic attacks on the deplorable state of society and double morality in *The Apartment* (1960).

population attended one movie per week—in all, over four billion tickets were sold.

Hollywood flooded the eager European market with its products until several European governments, worried about their own local film industry, introduced import restrictions and forced the Americans to invest a part of their export profits in European productions, as well.

But even before the end of the decade, there were dramatic decreases in attendance. The men who were returning from the war and the women who had taken on jobs outside the home during the war now retreated into private life. They moved from the cities to the suburbs, started families, and had no time for the cinema, which was less easily accessible than before.

The market leaders suffered a further blow besides the decrease in attendance. The courts analyzed Hollywood's finances and took decisive steps to free the film industry from the stranglehold of the large companies. In 1948, the Supreme Court found the eight largest studios guilty of monopolistic practices and forced them to separate from their cinema chains. Another part of the Court's decision forbid the practice of block-booking, which required independent theater operators to accept entire groups of films sight unseen.

The judgments sealed the fate of the studios, whose entire economic base rested upon the principle of a stable and calculable sales market. The studios could no longer finance their production apparatus with high costs and multiple personnel, and at the end of the 1950s evolved more and more

into powerful media concerns. The breakup of the studio cartels seemed at first to have positive effects on film work, because it took power away from the conglomerates and created space for independent directors and authors. New tax laws were created in such a way that it was favorable for stars and star directors to produce on their own. If a company was formed for each film project, the profit brought by sale of the film to a distributor would only be taxed at 25 percent.

Between 1946 and 1956, the number of independently-produced films doubled annually. With this greater artistic freedom, directors gained in stature. They were discovered as the actual artists of the film and from that point on enjoyed the star status previously reserved only for actors and actresses.

The master of suspense

One of the most famous and successful directors, who after 1948 also produced his own films, was Alfred Hitchcock, who made his most important films during the mid-1950s. As a young director, Hitchcock had tried various genres, but soon he concentrated on only one genre, the thriller, which he dominated and developed like no one else. Hitchcock took personal pleasure in confounding his audience and aimed constantly at surprising them. His goal was not terror or horror, but "suspense." This particular form of tension arises when the

viewer, who knows something the character does not, emotionally and fervently hopes that the latter will discover the

Alfred Hitchcock (1899–1980) learned the craft of film in England from the ground up, working as director's assistant, script writer and set designer. For 50 years, between 1926 and 1976, he left his mark on film history with incomparably gripping and cinematically extraordinary original thrillers. After he first appeared before the camera in *The Lodger* (1926) due to a lack of extras, his brief appearance became an obligatory gag in all his films.

The limited visual field of a photographer (James Stewart), who observes his neighbor and a murder through his zoom lens from an immovable point, becomes the dominating perspective in *Rear Window* (1954), and identifies the hero's voyeurism with that of his audience.

The "master of suspense" occasionally allowed himself blatantly unbelievable scenes in order to increase the tension. In *North by Northwest* (1959), the evil doers try to shoot the fleeing hero (Cary Grant) from a fertilizer airplane.

fate hanging over him in time. Hitchcock's heroes are for the most part unassuming, average people, who are frightened by unexplained occurrences (*Dial M for Murder*, 1954), unwittingly caught up in crimes (*Strangers on a Train*, 1951), or in general suspected and accused (*The Wrong Man*, 1957). Self-doubt and suspicion lead them to the depths of their own natures. Hitchcock's films probed in this way at all the carefully kept deep secrets, repressed fears, and erotic fantasies of his audience.

Through the confrontation of the harmless average citizen with the dangers brewing beneath the surface of apparent normality, the master of the thriller unsettled his contemporaries to the very core and, at least in his early films, provided catharsis with satisfactory explanations and subtle humor. Hitchcock constantly took on new aesthetic challenges. In 1943, he cast together in a "Life Boat," for the entire length of a film, the survivors of an Allied ship with the U-boat commander who

In his later films, Hitchcock didn't necessarily explain the mysterious events or forces with which his average heroes were confronted. This was the case in the thriller bordering on horror film *The Birds* (1963), which suggests the motif of revengeful nature.

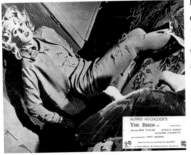

had torpedoed it, filming their unwelcome proximity in a compact sequence of suffocating close-ups. In *Rope* (1948), his first color film, Hitchcock used a moving camera to give the impression that it was filmed in just one sequence. Early on he was recognized as a skillful specialist of the unusually suspenseful criminal film; however, his films were not taken overly seriously by established reviewers. At the end of the 1950s the new French film critics, who were developing the *Nouvelle Vague*, discovered the artistic qualities of his films and venerated him, for his individual and innovative cinematic language, as "auteur." Hitchcock's idiosyncratic personal style, his detailed psychologizing of the typical thriller motifs, and last but not least, his masterful manipulation of the tools of the trade to produce suspense and surprise became trademarks for the suspense film genre and had considerable impact on the development of the cinema.

The great competition: television

After the film industry had been struck by the break-up of the cartels and the general decrease in attendance because of changes in the social structure, the introduction of television proved devastating. Its meteoric rise was without a doubt the main cause for the serious crisis of the cinema in the 1950s. The catastrophic decrease in attendance—between 1947 and 1951, the American cinema lost almost half of its viewers, and by 1957 approximately 75 percent—occurred parallel to the rising star of the new medium.

The war had only delayed the spread of television, which had been introduced in the 1930s. The electronics industry, which had been totally preoccupied with the manufacturing of war materials, began first, at the end of the 1940s, to balance out their over-capacity by mass manufacturing of television sets. The production-line manufacturing began in 1947, and by 1948 there were already one million sets in

The first CinemaScope film, *The Robe* (1953), used the overpowering visual impact of the wide-screen format to effectively stage mass and battle scenes. The box office hit prompted a barrage of very successful historical and Bible films, culminating in the historical spectacle *Ben Hur* (directed by William Wyler, 1959), which won 11 Oscars.

To project pictures in CinemaScope technique, the picture was compressed onto 35 mm film by means of a special anamorphic lens; the distortion was corrected during the projection again with an appropriate lens. Scene from *How to Marry a Millionaire* (1953) with Marilyn Monroe.

the United States. By 1960, television had entered 90 percent of all households.

In Europe, the same development occurred a little more slowly. From 1952 on, regular broadcasts were transmitted in Germany, leading to the disappearance of moviegoers there as everywhere else, and to the death of small cinemas. Like the cinema in 1895, television in 1947 seemed to fill a societal need and was immediately accepted. The new form of communication met the general desire for private, individual viewing as opposed to public. The cinema changed, as had the theater before it, from an everyday to a special leisure-time enjoyment. Viewers, who could watch everything presented to them on television, chose only specific films for their visits to the cinema. From that time on, going to the movies ceased to be a habit, and every film had to advertise with ever more elaborate promotional campaigns to draw its public into the theaters.

The first reaction of the film industry to the losses in attendance corresponded to this new behavior on the part of consumers: fewer films were produced, but those that were, were made more attractive movies based on famous novels and boasting star-studded casts.

Technical innovations

The film industry's reaction to this form of competition from the broadcasters of television was not purely negative. The idea of using television as a convenient new means of distribution for the countless, dust-covered feature films that were stored in

archives did not occur to anyone. Instead, the industry relied on the technical superiority of the cinema in comparison to the small, comparatively fuzzy TV picture of the era, and tried to build upon this advantage with technical innovations. The industry consciously promoted further development of the previously too-costly color films, which had not established themselves despite their public success at the end of the 1930s.

The development of color film

Hand coloring: Méliès and Edison had already used this procedure, in which the color is added after the fact with fine brushes to each individual frame of the completed film strip.

Virage: Almost all silent films up into the middle of the 1920s were tinted in at least two or even several colors through immersing them in a color bath. Generally blue tones were used for night scenes, red for fire, green for outside shots, and yellow for interior scenes. With the arrival of the sound film, this procedure disappeared, because the tinting bath damaged the soundtrack.

Tinting: Chemical coloring of black and white films, in which in contrast to the Virage color bath only the silver picture (that is the dark parts of the picture) accepted color. In combination with the Virage a two-color picture results.

Additive processes: During the exposure of a black and white film, individual pictures are prepared through filters, screens, or prisms for projection with different color lights. From red, blue, and green colored light during the projection, all the colors of the spectrum are mixed. The additive process forms the basis of color television; in the cinema, where it was first used in 1906 ("Kinecolor"), it was not able to establish itself.

Subtractive processes: Since white light is a mixture of all the colors of the spectrum, all colors can be reproduced on the screen with the aid of filters in the three basic subtractive colors yellow, cyanogen blue, and magenta red; in doing so, the different color shades on the films draw out the colors as needed from the white light projected through them. Subtractive processes established themselves in the late 1920s as opposed to the complicated and technically problem-prone additive processes.

Technicolor: Subtractive process which was first based on two (from 1917), then on three color separations (approximately from 1930). The color of the technicolor material is unsurpassed; famous technicolor films are *Gone with the Wind* (1939) and *An American in Paris* (1951).

Kodachrome: multi-layered film by Eastman (1950), in which three layers for the basic colors are directly transposed onto a single film strip which makes the material itself color sensitive.

Eastman color: In 1952 Eastman developed the Kodachrome process into a negative-positive process, which is today the standard for professional use.

Agfa color: A negative-positive color film developed in Germany, which differed from Eastman color only in the use of different coloring substances (color binders). The first evening length German color film was *Frauen sind doch bessere Diplomaten* (directed by Georg Jacoby, 1939)

3-D premier in New York, 1952.

In the early 1950s, the percentage of films made in color increased from 20 to 50 percent. In 1952, Eastman brought out a single-strip color film under the name "Eastman-Color," which, although not achieving the brilliance of the complicated three-strip technicolor process, made color film production and projection considerably easier. By the time television was able to broadcast in color in 1967, Hollywood had almost entirely switched over to color film.

The introduction of the wide screen caused a sensation. In 1952, Cinerama, a three projector system, celebrated its premiers. Even more successful was the less costly CinemaScope process which, with the aid of an anamorphic lens, compressed a wide-angle picture on a 35 mm film strip and decompressed it again during projection. In addition to color pictures and wide screen projection, the cinema fascinated the public with brilliant stereo sound. Film came closer and closer to reality.

Scented AromoRama films and Glorios-Smell-O-Visions, of course, were trends as short-lived as the 3-D cinema, which created the illusion of a three-dimensional picture with recognizable depth. The 3-D procedure relied upon the fact that our depth perception is a result of the distance between our eyes. This distance can be simulated by two cameras that simultaneously film one and the same scene at a distance of 5 cm from one another. This process had already been successfully used in stereo photography. So that all members of the audience in a large cinema could view these pictures from the same perspective, a polarized projection was introduced in the 1950s under the name "Natural Vision." People in the audience, who had to wear paper glasses with one red and one green lens, found this viewing aid burdensome and even complained about headaches. Besides, only a very few trendy films were made

Gene Kelly (1912–1996) was *the* musical star of the 1950s, along with Fred Astaire and Judy Garland. Among his greatest successes was the spirited comedy about the beginning of sound movies, *Singin' in the Rain* (1952).

with the 3-D process—a famous exception, by the way, was Hitchcock's *Dial M for Murder*—so that the technical innovation acquired the reputation of offering only cheap effects instead of the hoped-for exciting entertainment.

Improving the quality of the genre film

The attempts to improve the quality of the film itself proved beneficial especially to the tried-and-true classical genres such as the musical and the western, which owe some of their primary examples to the 1950s. Both genres profited from color and the wide screen; the western was enhanced by fascinating landscape shots, and the musical producers could put decorative and ornamental elements to use more effectively in their glamour films.

Fred Zinnemann's super western *High Noon* (1952) can be understood as a parable of the McCarthy era, in which no one dares to publicly support those who have been denounced and attacked.

Even the costume and historical spectacles owed their renaissance in the 1950s to the technical innovations made in film itself, for which the opulent monumental films were an effective means of display. Especially popular were epics whose story line stemmed from biblical sources. *The Ten Commandments* (1957) is one of the typical remakes of this decade,

which Cecil B. DeMille, apparently at the wish of his fans, was able to produce in CinemaScope with a gigantic budget, for its day, of 13 million dollars.

Freed from the narrow conventions of cheap B-picture production, the classical genres became more complex and exceeded their long-standing, clearly defined limitations. The break with traditional conventions opened up new aesthetic possibilities: the criminal film developed into the psycho-thriller, some musicals even became political satires, and the "super western" surprised audiences with its more individual character sketches and critical reflections on pressing societal problems. As a mirror of American society of the 1950s, the western raised

People invested in the genre of melodramas with great success. Men bearing psychological scars and brave, suffering women endure tragic blows of fate while being draped in expressive colors and revealed in merciless mirrors. Douglas Sirk created a masterpiece of the genre with the racial drama *Imitation of Life* (1958).

questions about the relationship between law and morality, the price of progress in civilization, the tensions between individual demands for happiness and societal restraints, and also addressed racism and tolerance of minorities.

One group of comedies was also relatively successful, taking the male image to the absurd. In the comedies of the duo Dean Martin and Jerry Lewis, for example, men appear as impractical and bungling, while decisive women move the plot forward.

The reduced production of films resulted in the disappearance of the *film noir*, whose specific aesthetics could not be realized in color. Only a star director like Hitchcock could allow himself to film a black and white film without a star cast in 1960. The extraordinary thriller *Psycho* became a cult film because of its mixture of grotesque comedy with elements of the horror genre.

Here come the kids

In an effort to counteract the competition of the attractive and convenient consumption of television programs, the film industry finally began to tailor its offerings to specific target groups. The large premier movie houses were turned into centers with many

Drive-in theaters boomed in the 1950s: there were just 24 "flickering parking lots" in 1945, but by 1956 the number had increased to 4,000, and they took in one quarter of the total film revenues for that year. One drawing card was the low admission price, and the fact that several films were usually shown during an evening. Drive-in showing of DeMille's *The Ten Command-ments*.

smaller theaters, which could simultaneously offer a wider array of films targeted for different age groups.

Hollywood produced cinema for the entire family, child stars experienced a boom, and advertising hype was directed deliberately along less scandalous paths. Films such as *Father of the Bride* (1950), *Cheaper by the Dozen* (1950), and *Houseboat* (1958) attempted to attract the different generations, who sat together all evening long in front of the TV, to the cinema with an idyllic picture of family happiness. Walt Disney specialized in entertainment and adventure films for children and youngsters. But the film industry's most important discovery was the youthful public.

While the grown-ups preferred to spend their free time in front of the TV, the more fun-loving teenagers were attracted to the inner cities, especially to darkened movie houses where they could not only enjoy the films which catered especially to their interests, but also do so in unobserved proximity to the opposite sex. Teenagers particularly valued the privacy of numerous drive-in theaters, or "passion pits," as they were called, whose rapid spread in 1950s coincided with the closing of traditional theaters. At the end of the 1950s, two-thirds of all movie-goers were between the ages of 16 and 24. The new composition of the public, of course, changed the content of the films as well. Teenage interest in the cinema was primarily for what television did not offer them: rock and roll musicals, horror and action films, and films that dealt with themes

In spite of (or perhaps partly due to) his tragic death at the age of 24, having made just three films, James Dean (1931–1955) became the embodiment of rebellious youth in a monotonous and indifferent adult world. After *East of Eden* (directed by Elia Kazan, 1954), and *Rebel Without a Cause* (directed by Nicholas Ray, 1955) followed *Giant* (directed by George Stevens, 1955), in which the foundering hero is stylized as the crucified Jesus next to Elisabeth Taylor in the posture of a kneeling Mary Magdalena.

Around the world, masses of young people flocked to movie theaters to see the "King of Rock 'n' Roll" sing on screen, although his films received mostly very negative critiques. *Jailhouse Rock* (1957).

such as juvenile delinquency and conflict between the generations.

European film artists

Despite all artistic, technical, and economic efforts, the American cinema during the 1950s suffered an irreversible decline. Actual innovations were taking place elsewhere. In Europe, measures taken against the competition of television and the dominance of Hollywood created favorable climate for the re-emergence of the cinema. In England and France, where the film industry was languishing after the war, the attempt was made to defend it against the flood of Hollywood productions through measures such as import quotas and special taxes. When the Americans threatened a boycott, an agreement was reached that required a part of the profits to be reinvested in the local film industry.

In England, France, Italy, and Scandinavia, local production after 1950 was able to register considerable increases. The upswing was further promoted by state support, co-productions with television, and intentional establishment of cineophile film clubs and film festivals, which became important promotional tools for a new generation of film artists outside the commercial distribution system. The European countries discovered the film as a promising export commodity and developed the festivals of Venice (since 1932), Cannes (since 1946), Karlovy Vary (since 1946), Locarno (since 1946), Berlin (since 1951), and San Sebastian (since 1954), bolstering international sales markets. Filmmaking was divided into popular and elitist branches, the latter diverging from the mainstream, highly-produced genre to become a personal art form whose director was recognized as the actual author rather than the scriptwriter.

The French critic Alexandre Astruc demanded, in a manifesto in 1948, a cinema of the *caméra-stylo*, in which the film's director writes with the camera, as

Along with Italian neorealism films and quality romantic films from France, Europe's hottest star Brigitte Bardot (b. 1934) was a great favorite with the Americans in her first movie breakthrough *And God Created Woman* (1956).

an author does with his hand, in order to develop a cinematic language as complex as literary language. According to this concept, the art of the film would also become as personal as literature; technique, staff, and acting ensemble would become instruments in the creative hands of the directing artist. Even in America, where the industry tried to address new target groups with counter-strategies against television, market niches developed for cineasts. In 1950 there were already a hundred art film theaters in the United States, and by the middle of the 1960s, over 600 cinemas played to a cinephile public. They of course showed mostly imported films from Europe, where a series of directors had unveiled their talents under the newly favorable conditions for cinematic art.

Italy: Fellini and Antonioni

In Italy, Federico Fellini (1921–1993), who after several early neorealistic films turned away from that movement, developed his own personal style. He was regarded as an autobiographical filmmaker, whose films became more and more rich in extra-ordinarily imaginative fantasy and reflections from his own subjective world. Recurring themes were male sexuality as well as his distinctively Italian love/hatred for the Catholic Church and its representatives. High points in his creativity, besides the frequently honored *La Strada* (1954) are *La Dolce Vita* (1960), about the decadence of Rome's high society, and *8 1/2* (1962), Fellini's multifaceted (and autobiographical) portrait of a director who, his creative energy having run dry during the large-scale production he has attempted, lapses into a dream-world in which he encounters characters from his childhood and finally directs them in a surrealistic circus dance. It was vehemently criticized by the Vatican.

The rather pessimistic and intellectual films of Michelangelo Antonioni (b. 1912) offered a

The cinematic fairy tale *La Strada*, in which Fellini's wife, Giulietta Masina, played the female lead, became Fellini's first international success but was criticized by his former colleagues as a betrayal of neorealism.

significant contrast to the life-affirming and erotic spectacles of his countryman. His unusual style could already be observed in his early films, with his fleeting and complex camera work in *Story of a Love Affair* (1953), *L'Aventura* (1959), and *The Night* (1960), which relate mysterious and erotic tales from different levels of time and conciousness. In 1966, he produced for MGM in England a film entitled *Blow-Up*, which demonstrated the contradictions of the modern film industry within its own medium, and which inspired the next generation of young filmmakers with its exceptonal quietitude and openness. It was not until 1982 that Antonioni was able to match the international success of *Blow-Up* with his mature work, *Identification of a Woman*.

Bibi Andersson und Liv Ullmann were among the inner circle of excellent actors and actresses who made up Bergman's star ensemble. In *Persona* (1966) he presented a psycho-drama of exquisite artistic alienation: the two protagonists seem to fuse into different aspects of one personality.

Sweden: Bergman

The Swede Ingmar Bergman (b. 1918), who between 1945 and 1983 made no fewer than 45 full-length films, had already been recognized in the 1950s, for his films *Smiles of a Summer Night* (1955), *The Seventh Seal* (1956) and *Wild Strawberries* (1957), as a pioneering film artist. All the way until his last great film *Fanny and Alexander* (1982), Bergman's works were marked with autobiographical details—his oppressive childhood in a strict household as the son of a Lutheran minister, his experiences in six marriages (particularly in *Scenes from a Marriage*, 1973), and his coming to terms with his role as an artist in society. Bergman's cinematic aesthetics were influenced by his background in the theater, which he never abandoned despite his success with films. Repeatedly using the same wonderfully synergetic ensemble of actors, he achieved psychological intensity in his cinematic chamber plays through the use of extreme close-ups and long sequences of filming. Bergman wrestled with moral and religious questions in his films, which also contributed, along with his reputation as a theater artist, to the fact that Western intellectuals began to observe the cinema as a serious art form befitting the times. With his image as a sensitive and uncompromising filmmaker, Bergman became a model for a new generation of directors; his films assumed a central position in the art film movement of the postwar era.

France: Tati and Bresson

In France in the 1950s, two innovative filmmakers entered the scene. Jacques Tati (1908–1982) and Robert Bresson (b. 1907) had comparatively nominal effects on the history of film but nevertheless left enduring works of art. Tati was also the main actor in his satiric comedies about the character M. Hulot, who confronts the fast-paced and treachery technology-filled everyday life in a world without human warmth. The many visual gags are unique to Tati's films, with their choreographed movement of figures, complex textures of funny noises, music and pointed dialog, as well as the director's tendency to use medium shots to underscore the friction between character and surroundings.

In his role as the quiet Monsieur Hulot, Jacques Tati's satires of the modern consumeristic society are reminiscent of the great tragic comedies of the silent film artists. Scene from *My Uncle* (1958).

Robert Bresson conceived of film as a mixture of

painting and music rather than of theater and photography, and spoke strongly on the behalf of Astruc's call for the *caméra-stylo*

With the spare style of his film *Diary of a Country Priest* (1950), Bresson revolutionized the cinematic language of his time. He eliminated all superfluous details from both actions and images, sometimes simply showing the writing hand of the protagonist for long moments.

aesthetic. His films were often based on famous literary sources but told in an entirely individualized cinematic language, which relied upon formal discipline, concentration on the essential, realistic simplicity of the pictures and rejection of manipulative effects such as underlying music or emotive acting. His actors were often non-professionals, whom Bresson treated as elements of the picture and not as artistic participants. Nevertheless, at the center of his stories were sensitive human beings who, in conflict with an alien environment, either mature or—especially in his later films—despair at the inhumanity of modern society and fail.

Japan

When a Japanese film surprised everyone by winning the Golden Lion of Venice in 1951, international interest turned for the first time toward Asia. *Rashomon* (1950) also received the Oscar for the best foreign film in 1952 and made its director Akira Kurosawa (*1910) an overnight international success. Until that point, the West had hardly taken notice of the rich tradition of the Asian cinema, which was highly developed in Japan and India. With the westernization of Japanese culture, brought by the rebuilding of Tokyo after the great earthquake of 1923, the cinema had been able to establish itself by the 1930s as part of everyday life in Japan. In the 1950s, Japan controlled the single market not dominated by Hollywood.

The highly stylized *Noh* and *Kabuki* theaters of Japan, steeped in ancient traditions, had only minor influence on the development of Japanese film. From the beginning, "modern films" (*gendai-geki*) with contemporary themes were made. In the 1930s, the directors of the genre took increasingly critical positions on corruption and capitalism and placed traditional values in question. Under pressure of increasingly reactionary politics and isolation during

In *The Castle of the Spider's Web* (1957). Kurosawa transported William Shakespeare's *Macbeth* into the world of Japanese knights and connected Western literary tradition with ritualized means of representation borrowed from *Noh* theater. In so doing, he created an epic of overwhelming visual power and cross-cultural ethical significance dealing with the basic issues of power struggles and repression of the powerless.

he Second World War, many activist artists gave way
o the less risky genre of the historical epic (*jidai-
eki*), treating actual, contemporary conflicts in the
uise of the *samurai* and sword-fighting stories that
ere popular with the public. With this typically
apanese genre, they supported the Japanese cinema
gainst the flood of Hollywood films during the
merican occupation and promoted independent
arrative style and techniques, which, though
nfluenced by Western conventions, still maintained
heir own, unique character. Thus *Rashomon*
urprised the Western public, not only by the plot set
n the Japanese Middle Ages but also through the
aring retrospective narrative technique of the story,
bout the death of a *samurai* and the rape of his wife,
resented in four different perspectives. The end left
pen the question as to whose
ersion of events was the true one—
hat of the bandit, the victim, his
vife, or an accidental eyewitness.

Kurosawa, who studied paiting and worked as an illustrator, is not only a gifted storyteller but also an excellent technician. The fight scenes so typical of his films have a particular dynamic achieved through time-lapse and telephoto shots. Color and its use to create rich images have been a central aesthetic feature of his work since the 1970s. Scene from *Kagemusha* (1980).

Kurosawa is considered the most
Western among Japanese directors,
nd he himself acknowledged the
nfluence of directors like Ford,
Hawks, Gance, Capra, and Wyler on
is work. One of his first
nternational successes, *The Seven
amurai*, whose title characters
acrifice themselves to save a village
rom bandits, is reminiscent of the
eroic humanism of the classic
vesterns. Many of his films are
dapted from Western literature,
uch as *The Lower Depths* (1957),
rom Gorki's play of the same name,
The Idiot (1951) from the novella by
Dostoevski, and *Ran* (1985) from
Shakespeare's *King Lear*.

Other Japanese directors besides
Kurosawa won international acclaim

In his contemporary socio-critical films, Kenji Mizoguchi addressed himself primarily to the fate of repressed Japanese women as, for example, in *Women of the Night* (1948), a portrait of the lives of prostitutes.

in the 1950s. Kenji Mizoguchi (1898–1956) and Yasujiro Ozu (1903–1963), who have been among the most important film artists of Japan since the 1920s, filmed a series of movies in the 1950s which have become classics of the world's repertoire. Their films were more clearly Japanese than those of Kurosawa, concerning themselves exclusively with material from Japan's present and past and its own cultural tradition. Their style was rather meditative, their pictures unfolding in slow tempo with extended takes, while Kurosawa's work, for example, was known for abrupt shifts out of slow motion and lightning-fast edited sequences.

India: Satyajit Ray

India can look back on a long and productive history of film like few other developing countries. After Lumières' travelling projectionists brought the new medium to Bombay as early as 1896, the travelling cinemas soon reached even the smallest villages, so that film soon became the most important form of entertainment for the mostly illiterate masses.

Popular from the very beginning were films whose superficial plots, most often re-tellings of the adventures of important Hindu heroes in *Rāmāyana* and *Mahabharata*, merely provided a loose backdrop for a string of 16 to 18 dance and musical numbers.

'his recipe for success, which had already etermined Indian theater for centuries, is even oday being used as a template for countless films— ndia has been the country with the most volu- ninous annual film production since 1971. Around ·50 movies are made in the celluloid-metropolis of ßombay alone each year, which means that "Bolly- vood" has an output four times greater than that of Hollywood.

Only a few outstanding films can be singled out of his massive production. The art of Indian cinema irst attracted international attention in the 1950s vith the works of Satyajit Ray (1921–1992), who, nfluenced by the Italian neorealists and Jean Renoir, iecame an important chronicler of the transforma- ions India went through between its traditional

The Chess Players (1977) by Satyajit Ray portrays two Indian noblemen in the 19th century who are so focused on their passion for the game of chess that they forget every- thing around them, even ignoring the British occupation of their country.

oots and its development as a modern capitalistic ountry. As an author, composer and director in one, Ray is in many ways typical of European-influenced *iuteurs*—the majority of his film productions were ;ubsidized, and were made without regard for their ommercial success. Aesthetically, as well, his films, ncluding the neorealistic *Father Panchali* (1955), the iolitical *Days and Nights in the Forest, Two* (1969), the he historical Hindi epoch film *The Chess Players* 1977), bear greater resemblance to European artistic ïlms than to the highly stylized, commercially ;uccessful entertainment cinema.

In 1908, when the first full-length films were made, the production of a feature film cost approximately two hundred dollars and lay in the hands of a single filmmaker who usually signed simultaneously as producer, writer, director, and sometimes even cameraman, and who also had control over pre-production, i. e., the casting and the writing of the script, as well as the post-production—the editing and special effects of the film. The financial disaster of David W. Griffith's *Intolerance* (1916) led to financial backers first withdrawing financial control from the directors and imposed upon them an "executive producer," who watched over the progress of their work as well as over their expenditures.

By the middle of the 1920s, when Hollywood was producing films *en masse*, the work was divided up among specialists, much as in industrial production after the introduction of the conveyor belt. The director as well as the camera man now had a limited number of tasks to perform and also limited power to make decisions. The set director, whose work corresponded to that of the stage director in the theater, the costume and makeup people, and the lighting technician also assumed important functions in the production team. Griffith, the director of the first American

full-length film, already had a cutter on his production staff who cut the film scenes to the desired length and spliced them together into the final version of film. However, the final aesthetic decision as to which scenes would be spliced into longer sequences—the montage work—was the province of the director, who, like Sergei Eisenstein, the pioneer of film montage, often took care of the editing work himself.

Many new occupations developed in the wake of technical progress. First, the introduction of sound film and the resulting film dialogue with it made necessary the collaboration of a scriptwriter. During the silent film era, there was hardly a director to be found who had worked with a written script that went beyond a short plot outline. Writers were, at best, there to offer suggestions. Silent film comedians, accustomed to improvising their slapstick comedy on set, vigorously rejected script requirements that could have restricted their spontaneity.

The collaboration of well-known authors from theater or from the literary world not only contributed to enhancing respect for cinematic art but also guaranteed the producers a greater control over the pro-uction, which, with rising osts, carried greater and greater nancial risks for the film ompanies. The more costly the roductions became, the more imited the artistic freedom of he filmmakers. The directors, who were progressively down-raded to the status of mere echnicians among a growing roduction team, had input, at est, only in the artistically mportant decisions such as asting, but the final cut was nade in the end by the pro-ducers and financial backers. ven today, it is considered a pecial privilege when a director etains the right of the final cut, nd it is a cinematic event when he director's cut, the version uthorized by the director, ventually makes it into the heater. Ridley Scott surprised he public in 1993 with his director's cut of *Blade Runner* 1982); the disturbing off-ommentary of the first version vas removed and the awkward happy ending left open.

After the collapse of the great studios, in which stars and directors had been as much a part of the permanent ensemble as the technical collaborators and were themselves under the power of the tycoons for better or for worse, the independently operating artists again gained greater influence over film production. The 1948 decision to dismantle the cartels wrested from the studios their former control over distribution. This cleared the way for directors as well as actors to produce films as well, without needing the approval of the majors to show their films in any movie theater. Even if they continued to work for the studios, they could now demand higher salaries and a

most essential part of pre-production along with the casting of the actors and the igning of the technical crew is the acquisition of a promising subject and a good script. n entire team usually works up the plot sketch, down to the treatment at the scene evel, and divides up the work into special areas, such as love scenes or action scenes. or animated films and films with a high degree of special effects, such as *Jurassic Park*, additional drawn story boards are prepared.

During filming day on the set at any one time, there are sometimes up to a hundred staff-members standing around the director: from the sound director to the cameramen, the camera crane operators, lighting specialists, lighting doubles and sound technicians; from the set directors, set builders and prop people down to wardrobe people, hair stylists, and make-up people; from the animal trainer to the press liaison; from the stunt man to the person in charge of under-age actors, who all of course have their assistants at their side.

greater influence on shaping the final version of the film. Already in 1947, Alfred Hitchcock separated himself from his producer David O. Selznick and from then on produced and directed one film per year until 1960. He bought the rights to stories, contracted actors from the free market, and had a large, permanent working staff at his disposal. James Stewart was the first actor to negotiate a percentage with his studio (Universal), something quite sensational in the 1950s.

Along with the stars, agents also developed influence in Hollywood, because they conducted negotiations with the film companies. Their power grew simultaneously along with the number of famous actors, directors, and scriptwriters, whom they represented. The agents preferred to represent them not as individuals but in so-called package deals they tried to sell for the production of a film.

Today, for the most part, it is the independent producers who produce a set number of films within a previously determined budget for the film studios, which have developed into large media concerns. To ensure financing, the film companies, who reserve all the rights for themselves, simultaneously conclude contracts with investors, who front the production costs and in return enjoy the profits within a set period of time of about five years. If during the course of these contracts the film does not cover its production costs, the studio pays back the investors after deducting a previously determined amount for the development of the project.

The level of budgeting for a film depends most decisively upon the attractiveness of the package that producers may assemble from a promising subject matter, a proven scriptwriter, the most popular stars, and a both famous and experienced director, who can bring the entire team to its fullest potential. Today, not only artists are hired from the free market. The producer leases or buys for each individual project the technical equipment and signs up mera teams, technicians, cutters, t directors, and special effects xperts from independent firms ho work at the highest possible andard.

Anyone striving today to roduce a blockbuster that will ank among the all-time hits has to nvest around a hundred million ollars for production. This is the inimum necessary if the script is o be adapted from a best-selling ovel by an author such as Michael richton (*Jurassic Park* and *The ost World*, 1993/1997); or if the ead role is to go to a star like om Hanks (*Forrest Gump*, 1993), rnold Schwarzenegger (*The erminator* and *Terminator 2: Judgment Day*, 1990/1994), or Tom ruise (*Mission: Impossible*, 1996). ikewise, the directing will need to e done by, if not Steven Spielberg, ne of his proteges like Robert emeckis (*Back to the Future I–III*, 986/1990) or one of the promi-

sing new talents like Roland Emmerich (*Independence Day*, 1996) or James Cameron (*Titanic*, 1997), who is not particularly known for his budget restraint. Anyone then wanting to work with the trendsetters in the special effects business, George Lucas' firm "Industrial Light & Magic," for instance, can almost be assured of certain success. Public reaction and artistic achievement are, however, not 100 percent assured, as was shown by legendary flops such as *Cleopatra* with Elizabeth Taylor, which, with a budget of 44 million dollars nevertheless returned 34 million, while Michael Cimino's equally expensive *Heaven's Gate* only took in 1.5 million dollars. The greatest flop in the history of film, *Water World*, with Kevin Costner as director and star, could barely cover its 170 million dollar production costs after an especially bad start.

he introduction of the computer to the post-production phase as revolutionized work in the tudio: Enormous time is saved nd several edited versions can e produced simultaneously and ompared. The film negative self is only cut after the omputer copy. The new echnical possibilities of omputer animation are normous for producing special ffects which can be combined ith real film scenes during the igital composing process.

1961
Building of the Berlin Wall; the Russian Yuri Gagarin is the first man in space.
1962
Cuban missile crisis
1963
Assassination of John F. Kennedy
1964
Beginning of racial unrest in the United States
1965–1975
The Vietnam War
1966
Beginning of the Cultural Revolution in China
1967
Six-Day War in the Near East
1968
Assassination of Martin Luther King, Jr.
1969
Woodstock Festival; first landing on the moon
1973
Oil crisis; Watergate affair; military coup and assassination of President Salvador Allende in Chile

Between new directions and tradition

In the 1960s and 1970s, an atmosphere of fundamental cultural and political change gripped the world, and a pervasive change of values emerged. In the United States, the civil rights movement provided the impetus for a realignment of the social order among cultural minorities and the white Anglo-American majority. Because of active engagement against discrimination through protests against imperialism and demonstrations for peace and free love, not only by African-Americans but also by other minorities such as women and children, society gradually moved away from its traditional conception of morality and values.

A limited thaw in the Eastern Bloc countries, where large segments of the population demanded the democratization of socialism, paralleled this period of liberalization in the Western world.

The upheaval originated with the younger generations, whose rejection of the values of their parents overstepped the boundaries of the typical generational conflict. The youthful counter-culture of the 1960s was an international phenomenon and found its expression in the world-wide reach of rock and pop music, unconventional dress, the sexual revolution, experimentation with mind-altering drugs, and the testing out of new styles of communal life and work.

The rebellion of Western youth turned political with student revolts, which not only denounced the "thousand-year-old stench" of university education; it also saw itself as the nucleus of a movement which, carried forward equally by the educated class and the working-class, would replace capitalism and imperialism with socialism, peace, and a more just distribution of the world's wealth.

The dream of a new, enlightened, just and free world, however, burst quickly. The failure of alternative lifestyles at a time characterized by both economic recession and a restorative mood led the generation of 1968 in the 1970s, as adults, either to a resigned "march through the institutions" or to destructive terrorism, which accelerated the strengthening reactionary, anti-social, and military forces rather than inhibiting them.

An important influence of the civil rights movement on American film was the recognition that the cinema could not only portray reality, but also have an effect by virtue of its capacities to propagate and ingrain sexist and racist ideologies. African-American actors, for example, were cast in the 1960s only in subservient or comic roles and were only allowed to play dramaturgically necessary characters of their race. One of the first African-American stars was Sidney Poitier (b. 1927), who, in *In the Heat of the Night* (1966), plays a detective accused of murder.

Cinema's fundamental change

By the 1960s, at the latest, the cinema had to redefine and assert its position in a restructured media landscape, in which television now dominated as the primary leisure-time entertainment of the masses. Although the works of several outside directors had already managed in the 1950s to add the art film to the commercialized mainstream offerings of the cinema, it was the 1960s that allowed for the significant growth of art film movements. These set about eradicating the usual conventions of film creation scorned as "papa's cinema" and sought to enhance the stature of the film medium as an independent art form equal to the other traditional genres.

The new generation of filmmakers who belonged to these movements was no longer self-taught but had enjoyed technical and theoretical training at the national film academies founded in the mean time in different European countries. There they had intensively studied the films and work processes of their great predecessors— the German expressionists, the American masters of the genre film, and the Italian neorealists— and had at their disposal a profound treasury of

"How did you do it, Mr. Hitchcock?" asked one of the leading critics and directors of the French *Nouvelle Vague*, François Truffaut (1932–1984), the master of cinematic codes. The interview, published in book form, demonstrated the great veneration of movie innovators for the authors of the Hollywood film, whose conventions they wanted to master in order to break them.

specific cinematic codes with which they could experiment or dispense as they saw fit. The "new waves,"—"free cinema," "new cinema," and "young cinema"—ultimately brought an entirely different, predominantly young public to the theaters.

For the youth of the 1960s and 1970s, the cinematic film became the most popular, and even the exclusive, artistic medium; youth discussed film art more frequently than the traditional art forms of theater, literature, or the fine arts. The entirely discredited Hollywood film of the "sad sixties," the dullest period in the history of American film, was able to win back its leading position in the world market because it absorbed the impulses and innovations of these movements of the art film.

France: *Nouvelle Vague*

The striving toward a basic thematic and aesthetic new beginning was most noticeable in France, where cultural politics and film industry promoted, with an eye toward the future, innovative and artistically ambitious young talent. The establishment of a national fund to promote film-making contributed to this end, as did the active engagement of independent, adventurous producers along with the development of a broad base of over 400 cinematic art theaters.

The movement of the *Nouvelle Vague* itself derived ultimately from André Bazin's journal on film theory *Cahiers du cinéma*, in which a group of young critics analyzed the aesthetics and history of film. From the study of film classics and the analysis of the *film noir* and the old masters such as Renoir, Lang, and Hitchcock, they developed the tools to criticize the perfect but boring *cinéma de qualité* of their contemporaries.

The enthusiastic film fan François Truffaut set the tone; he castigated the prevailing cinema as one of stalled conventions and mass produced illusions, calling for cinematic experimentation instead. Truffaut propagated an "imperfect cinema of authors," which no longer denied the personal style and the individual outlook of its creators, the directors, but sought to elevate them into trademarks. The authors of the cinema, according to Truffaut, had to learn from literature instead of imitating it, and to work on the expansion and revival of the specific aesthetic means of their medium, i. e., on an "Ecriture filmique." In 1959 he introduced the prototype of the new cinematic art, *The 400 Blows*, which right away won the award for Best Direction at Cannes and, as a box-office success, helped smooth the way for future projects of his *Nouvelle Vague* colleagues. The autobiographical first film from Truffaut's *Antoine Doinel* cycle denounced the indifference and arbitrary educational methods of a generation of adults so concerned with all their own personal shortcomings that they stood helplessly by in the face of the needs of those entrusted to their care.

The casting of the role of the young Antoine, who had come upon hard times, with Jean-Pierre Léaud (b. 1944) for Truffaut's early masterpiece *The 400 Blows* proved to be a stroke of good fortune. Léaud became an overnight star and contributed to many important films after that under the direction of Godard, Pasolini, Cocteau, and Bertolucci among others.

His two following films, a parodic criminal film in the style of the *film noir* (*Shoot the Piano Player*, 1959/1960) and the equally poetic and tragic history of a love triangle (*Jules and Jim*, 1961/1962), anticipated the most important themes of the new French film.

The *Nouvelle Vague* was not a particularly unified movement or a school. The critics, who debuted one after the other as directors, saw themselves much more as autonomous artistic personalities and soon went their own artistic ways. Claude Chabrol (b. 1930), whose debut film *Scream If You Can* (1958) ranks among the biggest commercial successes of the *Nouvelle Vague*, dedicated himself

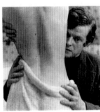

Eric Rohmer's film *Love in the Afternoon* (1972) is the last in a series of six "moral stories," each of which shows a new variation on the age-old story of a man between two women. Rohmer continues the sub-genre created by him successfully in the 1980s with a series of *comédies et proverbes*. His style has remained unchanged up to today: instead of plots he shows people who talk about love; his portraits are exceedingly intelligent and sensible, though ironically distanced, but never without respect.

first and foremost to the socially critical criminal film, while Eric Rohmer (b. 1920) repeatedly portrayed men and women in search of happiness and in the desperate balancing act between reason, emotion, and erotic drives. Jacques Rivette (b. 1928), who experimented with combining the feature and documentary film, worked—with inspiration from the theater—with improvisation in his often overly lengthy films, defined film as a system of symbols rather than as a narrative process.

The work of Jean-Luc Godard, the second key figure of the movement, marked the antithesis to the films of Truffaut within the *Nouvelle Vague*. While Truffaut was predominantly interested in a rejuvenation and renewal of traditional cinematic art, Godard worked persistently toward new definitions of cinematic structure and style. The most provocative and innovative among the proponents of the *Nouvelle Vague*, Godard broke with cinematic conventions, abandoned eventually in the course of his work the fictional coherence of plot, and turned to the form of the film essay. Already in his first feature film, *Breathless* (1959), he tested his public's entrenched way of seeing things, as well as their conditioning toward formal perfection, by violating cinematic conventions. This homage to the *film noir* went against the grain with multiple jump-cuts, or leaving out frames within a scene so that the public imagines the film is jumping and loses the sense of continuity during a scene. The film was striking in its lack of

Claude Lelouch's *A Man and a Woman* won the Golden Palm of Cannes in 1966 and was received enthusiastically by the public as well as by critics worldwide. Lelouch was responsible not only for production, script, and directing, but also for camera work and editing. The film tells, with expressive means (skillfully added color effects, sounds, and composites of pictures), a rather banal love story; the signature of its author was more responsible for its success than the story.

production technique, tripods, cranes, and tracks, and in the filming of actual Parisian location scenes with the more mobile hand camera. The semi-documentary introduction of candid scenes from everyday life was a stylistic device used in many films of the *Nouvelle Vague*.

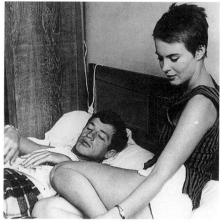

The extraordinary success of *Breathless* made Jean-Paul Belmondo (b. 1933) France's film darling overnight. The film tells the story of a small-time crook who, in his attempts to imitate his movie idol Humphrey Bogart, increasingly loses contact with reality and—after his girlfriend betrays him—dies a movie hero's death while fleeing the police.

The cinematographer Raoul Coutard (b. 1924), who, following the success of *Breathless*, became one of the most sought-after collaborators of the *Nouvelle Vague* directors, brought to feature films the aesthetics of the *cinéma vérité*, the progressive French documentary film of the 1960s. At the end of the 1960s, after a series of films revolving around the difficulties of men and women living together (for example, *Contempt*, 1963) and more strongly focused on the mechanics of narration than upon story itself, the unorthodox Marxist turned away from the analysis of cinematic forms to occupy himself with political questions in *La Chinoise* (1967) and *Weekend* (1967).

The *Nouvelle Vague* met an early end at the Cannes Festival in 1968 when its main proponents Godard, who had become increasingly involved in the student revolts, and Truffaut, who was tending

Although Jean-Luc Godard (b. 1930) withdrew for almost the entire decade of the 1970s from the cinema, experimenting instead with television films and with the new video medium, he has influenced the modern cinema as scarcely anyone else has. Only in the 1980s did this proponent of the *Nouvelle Vague* return to the cinema and make a mark with his intelligent and sensual reflections on the language of pictures and the complex business of the filmmaker and purveyor of illusions in films such as *Passion* (1982), *The Splendor and Misery of a Small-Time Movie Concern* (1984), and *Nouvelle Vague* (1989).

Important impulses for the modern art cinema came from Alain Resnais, who stands closer to the avant-garde authors of the *Nouveau Roman* than to the *Nouvelle Vague*. In *Hiroshima, mon amour* (1959) he linked the love between a French woman and a Japanese man with atomic genocide. The film was extremely innovative in its use of contrapuntal balance of words, music, and pictures, and mixed the time frames by not differentiating remembered scenes of the heroine's earlier love for a German occupation officer from the present time of the story.

The changeover from the cumbersome 35 mm camera to more flexible 16 mm camera permitted the directors of the free cinema to film many scenes at real city locations so that the industrial landscapes of Manchester and Salford became important components of the new realism. Scene from *The Loneliness of the Long-Distance Runner*.

more toward mainstream cinema, became embroiled in a fight.

England's free cinema

A long-lasting revitalization of the English cinema came about from a group of young artists who presented six programs of social documentary short films in London's National Film Theatre between 1956 and 1959 under the title free cinema.

The British Film Institute supported production and presentation of programs, which, along with films of young British directors such as Tony Richardson (1928–1991), Karel Reisz (b. 1926), and Lindsay Anderson (b. 1923) were supposed to make films from France, America, and Poland accessible to a wider public—among them those of the Polish Roman Polanski. Theoretical manifestos accompanied the rebellion against the constraints of the commercial and conservative cinema industry. The filmmakers attempted to redefine the societal responsibility of the artist and called for a cinema that presented the problems of everyday life, especially those of the

working-class. However, in contrast to the British documentary film of the 1930s and 1940s, which had focused on changes in the working world due to the increase in technology, the free cinema movement was interested especially in the youthful subculture which came about as a result of the social change of the new affluent society.

After the success of semi-documentary short films, the

leading directors of the free cinema soon turned to feature film production. They were inspired essentially by the contemporary literature of the "angry young men," unadorned excerpts of "real life" from the pen of Alan Sillitoe, John Osborne, and many others. As on

Lindsay Anderson's short film *Thursday's Children*, which won an Oscar in 1954, portrayed the everyday life of deaf children.

the London stage, the cinema now also showed, for the first time, people who had to earn their livelihood, sleep together, and get drunk.

After a short New Wave, the distinctions between free cinema and commercial feature film became blurred with the notable filming of socially critical literature, such as *Look Back in Anger* (1959) adapted from John Osborne and *The Loneliness of the Long-Distance Runner* (1962) adapted from Alan Sillitoe (both under the direction of Tony Richardson), as well as Karel Reisz's public success *Saturday Night and Sunday Morning* (1960), also adapted from Sillitoe. In 1964, the most productive director of the group, Tony Richardson, was awarded an Oscar for the box office success *Tom Jones* (1962, adapted from Fielding), a turbulent and sensuous parody of the classical adventure film.

Off-Hollywood

Hollywood continued to dominate American cinema to such a degree that, in the 1960s especially, an active avant-garde could scarcely be detected. Avant-garde filmmakers, who joined together to form the underground movement in New York, were united less by a common style than by the need to band together against censorship, police raids, and disparagement by the press. Even tame films had to be shown occasionally in secret, because the police repeatedly seized experimental and political film reels and arrested the organizers of showings.

Among the most famous of the censored films of the underground is Jack Smith's *Flaming Creatures* (1963), which stages a wild orgy with several women and a number of transvestites in a Manhattan department store. The New York City police destroyed all the copies of the film that fell into their hands. Years later it served as evidence in a trial opposing film censorship.

What was it that made the work of the avant-garde so suspicious and dangerous in the eyes of the protectors of morality and law? The young East Coast directors, who had learned to appreciate the European art film in film clubs and art theaters, had set out to undermine Hollywood's stake in the industry and its domination over a cinema which ran counter to public morals with provocative and innovative films.

On the West Coast in the 1960s no outsider, no matter how talented, had a chance. The smoothly crafted mainstream cinema became standardized to create the greatest possible appeal; aesthetic innovation seemed too risky to the producers. "We don't want any fake, polished, glossy films—we want them rough and unpolished but full of life. We don't want any rosy films—we want them in the color of blood!" proclaimed the New American Cinema Group, which was founded at the end of the 1960s in order to promote the financing and distribution of feature-length experimental films.

Shirley Clarke's *Cool World* (1963) portrayed the survival of young criminals in the Harlem ghetto.

The avant-garde was divided into two camps. One group of filmmakers remained true to the narrative feature film and worked on a new realism that was supposed to return the false cinematic picture of America and of its citizens back to real life from Hollywood triviality. Their films showed an unkempt America and did not shy away from a socially-conscious examination of the shadowy sides of the free market economy.

Lionel Rogosin (b. 1924) portrayed, in *The Bowery* (1955), the infamous New York street of the rejected and the failed; Shirley Clarke (b. 1925) in *The Connection* (1960) filmed a piece of living theater about African-American junkies. John Cassavetes (1929–1989), probably the most famous director in the underground, denounced racist discrimination in everyday life in *Shadows* (1960). The film met with accolades at numerous festivals and even achieved commercial success.

Under the influence of the avant-garde in literature, theater, new music, performance, and happenings, a different group of underground filmmakers helped bring the abstract, absolute "film as film" to a renaissance. The most prominent representative was Andy Warhol (1927–1987), the star of the pop-art movement.

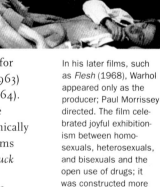

In his later films, such as *Flesh* (1968), Warhol appeared only as the producer; Paul Morrissey directed. The film celebrated joyful exhibitionism between homosexuals, heterosexuals, and bisexuals and the open use of drugs; it was constructed more conventionally and became a box office success.

His static films showed hour-long scenes, for example, of a sleeping man in *The Sleep* (1963) or the Empire State Building in *Empire* (1964). In later films, he broke out of this abstruse aesthetic and provoked audiences with ironically pointed, obsessively pornographic short films such as *Kiss* (1963), *Blow Job* (1964), and *Fuck* (1968).

Socio-critical realism, drastic portrayal of sexuality, and the nihilism of abstract "anti-action"—all forms of the underground cinema—revealed aspects of American reality consistently ignored by Hollywood. The open animosity against the underground movement demonstrated the

degree to which the anti-cinema attacked the aesthetics of the dream factory, which were removed from reality, along with its basic conviction, the unshakable, deeply rooted belief of American society in the "American dream."

Alexander Kluge (b. 1932), the cultural politics head of the *auteur* film, continues to be a tireless fighter for a critical film and TV artform in Germany. In his films, he uses an unconventional "open" narrative form, which demands the intellectual involvement on the part of the viewer, and takes a position on political situations in West Germany, as, for example, in his film *Artists at the Top of the Big Top: Disoriented* (1968), which premiered in Venice in 1968 and was a renunciation of overachievement in our society.

The Oberhausen manifesto

Fascism and war in Germany led first to an abrupt end of artistic development and eventually to the total demise of the existing film industry. Studios and cinemas were destroyed; people connected with movies were politically incriminated. With the gradual resumption of production of entertainment films which were totally non-political—operettas, social comedies, the doctor, artist, and *heimat* film—the German film economy was able to satisfy the local market but could not compete on the international level.

When the television crisis set in at the end of the 1950s, considerably weakening the German film industry, the West German government jumped into the breach with subsidies, tax relief, and favorable credits. Thus the collapse of commercial film production indirectly worked to the advantage of a new generation of filmmakers, who set about offering an alternative to the dominant average film and the prevailing blood-and-soil ideology. In 1962, 26 young directors, inspired by the *Nouvelle Vague*, signed a manifesto at the short-film festival in Oberhausen, in which they declared "papa's cinema" dead and raised the demand for "... a new German feature film. This new film needs new freedoms. Freedom from the usual industry conventions. Freedom from the influence by commercial partners. Freedom from the patronization of interest groups. We have concrete, intellectual, formal, and economic ideas about the production of the new German film."

The climate for the realization of these goals was created in 1965 by the founding of the Curatorium of Young German Film. With tax money running into the millions, the first independently-produced films were financed, and soon international successes arose. Alexander Kluge's *Yesterday Girl* won a Silver Lion in 1966 in Venice, and the special award of the Berlin Film Festival was granted in the same year to Peter Schamoni's *Schonzeit für Füchse* ("Close Season for Foxes," 1965/66). Volker Schlöndorff's *Young Törless* (1965) was awarded the International Critics' Award in 1967 in Cannes.

Hunting Scenes from Lower Bavaria (directed by Peter Fleischmann, 1968) is an example of a series of "leftist *heimat* films," in which young *auteurs* used elements of the popular genre in provocative ways in order to get behind the issues of German identity and the concept of *heimat* ("homeland") from a critical perspective.

What united the movement of Young German Film was less a common aesthetic style than the determined reorientation toward societal themes. As before in England and France, the German public was again able to confront reality: the young filmmakers described West Germany as a country of disrupted marriages, reactionary parents, and rebellious youth in the desperate struggle to adapt to the new prosperity of the consumer society. It became possible for German *auteurs* to explore new subject matter arising from the new literature of West Germany, such as novels by Böll and Grass, and the always-recurring question of to what extent the fascist German past continued to live on in the democratic present.

The filmmakers attempted to demonstrate the critical distance from depicted reality through breaks in the conventions of cinematic narration. In particular, Alexander Kluge and Jean-Marie Straub (b. 1933) experimented with open and

The terrorism debate of the 1970s was reflected in films such as *The Lost Honor of Katharina Blum* (1975) by Volker Schlöndorff (b. 1939) and Margarethe von Trotta (b. 1942). It is the story of an non-political, defenseless servant girl, who, because of her acquaintance with a falsely presumed terrorist, is victimized by police, the justice system, and an unscrupulous, sensationalist press.

playful forms in their films, using off-commentary and inserted text as alienating effects, and cut documentary and fictional scenes in associated montages beside one another. They joined scenes from present and past, not in causal or chronological plot sequences but juxtaposed directly next to one another, thereby demanding a real effort on the part of their public to reconstruct the meaning.

New German film

Toward the end of the 1960s, a second generation of directors arose who continued the socially critical impetus of the New German Film and radicalized it as part of a growing counter-culture and of the new left.

Political involvement reached a high point in 1978 with a collective project, *Germany in Autumn*. Nine directors reacted, in this cooperative feature, to the mood in West Germany after the Schleyer kidnapping and the suicides of the terrorists arrested in Stammheim. The film exemplifies the turning away of the left from political activism toward a strategy of the "long march through the institutions," presenting at the same time a sampling of the broad stylistic spectrum of the New German Film.

Germany in Autumn prompted a series of film projects which dealt with different pictures of Germany and examined the roots of the present-day crisis of that time in the fascist past.

The search for German identity

One of the most prolific among the new German filmmakers was Rainer Werner Fassbinder (1946–1982), who, with over 30 films, assumes a central position among filmmakers of the '60s and '70s. He also became one of the most controversial and famous figures of the cinema scene, owing to his self-destructive lifestyle as well as his work style, in which he joined life and art in assembling a permanent staff of collaborators and actors as an ensemble in the creative process. In *Beware the Holy Whore* (1970), Fassbinder analyzed self-critically the impossibility of such collective filmmaking.

After a series of formally ascetic short films, Fassbinder worked vigorously at his own cinematic signature. He discovered, at the beginning of the 1970s, a spiritual father in the Hollywood star and master of the melodramatic genre, Douglas Sirk from Denmark. In his early feature films *The Merchant of Four Seasons* (1971) and *Fear Eats the Soul / Ali* (1973), Fassbinder consciously emulated stylistic elements of his model, featuring the melodramatic material with garish decor bathed in dramatic light, and using exposed camera movement, in a complex play of interpersonal identification and alienation. Both films stand out from Fassbinder's work, which confronts, as much concretely as critically, the less spectacular aspects of everyday life in West Germany.

At the end of the 1970s, Fassbinder shifted his efforts from the immediate present to the immediate past; in his German trilogy, he sought the causes for the problems of finding identity in West

Rainer Werner Fassbinder was not only the author and director of his films but also often appeared as an actor, as he did in *Fear Eats the Soul / Ali* (1973), the story of the love and marriage of a widow to a guest-worker twenty years younger than she.

Hans Jürgen Syberberg's *Hitler: A Film from Germany* (1978) is one of the most controversial cinematic treatments of Nazi Germany. While neglecting the political and economic factors that made it possible for fascism to succeed, the film attempted to approach the phenomenon of Hitler through an analysis of the irrational levels of the souls of the German people.

Germany in the reconstruction years between materialistic greed (*The Marriage of Maria Braun*, 1978), opportunistic adaptation (*Lola*, 1981), and the tormented reminders of a dramatic past which were repressed instead of being faced (*Veronica Voss*, 1981).

Fassbinder's development, from his early experimental and radically political works to films in which he expertly understood how to most effectively adapt Hollywood's cinematic conventions, reflects a general trend in the history of the New German Film. But Alexander Kluge, the most important theoretician of the movement, and Hans Jürgen Syberberg (b. 1935) broke with the laws of narrative in their films and rationally argued cinema. Volker Schlöndorff, Werner Herzog (b. 1942), and Wim Wenders (b. 1945) represented not only the commercial but also the more successful group, according to the international critics. They hoped to spread their political and societal activism by means of the large cinema, resulting in their international co-productions, since the 1980s, primarily outside of Germany.

Fassbinder's early death in 1982 was one mark of the end of the "German film miracle." German film productions succeeded almost exclusively on the German market, while internationally successful German filmmakers such as Wolfgang Petersen (*Das Boot*, 1981), Wim Wenders (*Paris, Texas*, 1984), and most recently Roland Emmerich (*Independence Day*, 1996) have established for themselves a firm place in Hollywood.

"I have forgotten the book and seen a movie," Günter Grass praised Schlöndorff's filming of his novel, *The Tin Drum* (1978). The film, which collected numerous awards, is seen as the model for the adaptation of a literary work and ranks among the classics of West German postwar films.

Feminist film

Notable in Germany is the prominence of films dealing with women. The politically activist feminist cinema is, of course, not just a purely German phenomenon. It is rooted in the changing status of women world wide during the 1970s as they began to conquer masculine domains, such as the arts, and to use them as means of expression for a feminine aesthetic and world-view. The mass medium of the film served as the most broad-based, political tool for enlightenment. Germany's comprehensive promotion of film made it more possible for women to debut as directors than in other countries. First, documentary films about women were produced which revealed discrimination and called for solidarity in the struggle for emancipation. In contrast to the classical women's film by male directors, which at best psychologized the melodramatic genre depicting the tragic fates of women, feminist women's film re-politicized subjective experience by describing it as socially informed. The films of Helke Sander (*The Multisided Reduced Personality*, 1977; *The Subjective Factor*, 1981), Helma Sanders-Brahms (*Germany, Pale Mother*, 1979), and Margarethe von Trotta (*The German Sisters*, 1981) encouraged a search for feminine identity within a patriarchy and sought to make general observations about the relationship of private life and the politics beyond. Influenced by French film theory, the women directors defined feminist film art as counter-cinema to the male-oriented cinematic codes of Hollywood. Like the initiators of other avant-garde movements, they each sought artistic truthfulness and political expression in the break with the current narrative conventions and experimented with non-causal narrative forms that could reflect the disjointedness of real life experiences can be reflected.

Political cinema

While the new waves and movements in film were first concerned with aesthetic renewal, critical reaction to cinematic conventions, and the propagation of author films in contrast with the classic genre film, the end of the 1960s gave rise

There are few European directors who have dealt as intensively with America and Hollywood as Wim Wenders. *Paris, Texas*, an international co-production, presents a fascinating synthesis of American road film and European author movie.

to several filmmakers whose films were activist and political. The revolutions in the Third World, the Prague Spring, the politicalization of students, the protest of American youth against the Vietnam War, and the development of the "New Left," which demanded a social revolution, formed the core of a young political protest culture whose content and specific forms of expression re-sounded in contemporary artistic creations.

Pier Paolo Pasolini (1922–1975)

The Italian writer and theoretician from Friul had long been known in his novels and political poems for his strongly socialist utopian ideas, before he attacked in his films the *consumismo*, the consumer-oriented bourgeiosification of the revolutionary societal potential of the suburban poor as well as of the intellectuals. Even in his earliest films, Pasolini showed with *Accatone!* (1961) and *Mamma Roma* (1962) the hopeless-ness of striving for petit-bourgeois happiness. If these grim representations of life in the Italian suburbs seemed to be a call to social revolution, Pasolini created with his last film *Salo—The 120 Days of Sodom* (1975) a shocking, apocalyptic vision of the immutability of human barbarism in the midst of highly intellectual cultural refinement.

Stylistically, Pasolini remained tied to neo-realism up until his last film. He preferred to work with non-profes-sional actors, improvised on the set, and avoided narrative continuity in favor of complex expressive sequences of pictures and a specific montage technique, which he called *pasticchio*: The mixing of strongly contrasting visual and acoustical material. In *Salo*, he portrayed rape and torture scenes in classical picture com-position and under-scored them with music from Carl Orff's *Carmina Burana.*

Between these extremes of social engagement and pessimistic refutation at the immutability of the world, Pasolini nourished his unorthodox Marxist utopianism by setting it in a pre-civilized mythical milieu in films like *Oepidus Rex* (1967) and *Medea* (1969). His "trilogy of life" (*The*

Decameron, 1971, *The Canterbury Tales*, 1971, and *The Arabian Nights*, 1974) evolve into a celebration by the entire human race of fulfilling and shameless sexuality. His murder before the premiere of Salo brought his varied artistic and theoretical opus to a tragic and much too early end.

Cinema against repression

As Pasolini profited in Italy before the renaissance of the Italian film industry, other political and socially critical young filmmakers owe their international reputations to the economic and artistic strengthening of previously unnoticed cinematography from countries such as Greece, Poland, Turkey, and the countries of Latin America. There are interesting connections among traditions of the respective native cultures, film history,

Andrzej Wajda's passionate plea for democracy and human rights, *Man of Iron* (1981) told the story of a journalist who is given the assignment to report on the strike of the dock workers in Gdansk. When he realizes that his investigations are going to be used as material against the leaders of the strike, he switches over to the side of the workers. The film contained a series of original documentary footage of the historical events and even showed Lech Walesa in a minor role.

political involvement, and the specific signature of confident author filmmakers. The Greek Theodore Angelopoulos (b. 1936) dealt intensely and critically with the political development of his country and did not shun protesting, in his films, against the military dictatorship. His internationally admired *Traveling Players* (1975) tells the story of a group of traveling comedians who are repeatedly prevented from performing a harmless play, offering a paradigm for investigation of the structure of the Greek dictatorship between 1939 and 1952.

After all hope for democratization of socialism came to an end in Eastern Europe, with the suppression of the Prague Spring by Soviet troops, the most powerful political cinema came from Poland. The painter and film director Andrzej Wajda (b. 1926) had already turned away in the 1950s, with other directors of the Polish School, from the revolutionary optimism and positive heroes of the state-prescribed socialist realism. In the 1970s, he encountered great difficulties with the state censorship agencies, because, in his film *Man of Marble* (1976), he took an uncompromising look at Poland's Stalinist past and neo-Stalinist present, through the lens of a story of a "hero at work," which was extremely uncomfortable for the state and party apparatus. In 1981, he supported the activities of Solidarity with his internationally successful next film, *Man of Iron*, and, along with other young filmmakers, called for a new era of realistic cinema which would critically examine the present. The government, however, suppressed this movement with massive efforts and forced Wajda into artistic exile, from which he was unable to return to

In *Yol* (*The Way*, 1982) Güney depicted the experiences of various prisoners on furlough and showed strikingly how these men also experienced freedom in Turkey as a prison, whose walls consisted of conventional patriarchal concepts of honor and state repression.

his homeland until 1989, after the victory of Solidarity.

The military dictatorship in Turkey found its apparently most radical cinematic opponent in the director Yilmaz Güney (1937–1984), who achieved, in his country and as an extraordinary representative of its struggling cinematography, a position similar to that of Wajda. Before his career as an internationally successful director of Turkish film, Güney appeared as a popular actor in numerous commercial action films. The second film he directed, *Hope* (1970), was celebrated as the best Turkish film of all time because of its well thought-through, aesthetically composed images and suspenseful story.

After the military putsch of 1971, Güney was arrested again and again because of his candid social and political criticism, and in 1974, shortly after the completion of his critical portrayal of a Turkey entirely out of control (*The Friend*, 1974), was sentenced to 19 years in jail on trumped-up charges of murder.

Despite difficult conditions, Güney did not give up and completed his subsequent films from prison in collaboration with the director Zeti Ötken. In 1981 he escaped and thus was able to complete the film he had begun together with Serif Gören in French exile, *Yol* (*The Way*), his masterpiece that was awarded the Golden Palm in 1982. When Güney died of cancer in 1984, the Turkish government had all available copies of his films burned in an attempt to wipe out all traces of political dissidents. However, his contribution to a new, uniquely Turkish poetic realism is undeniable.

On the whole, the repressive state censorship in Turkey led to the world's greatest collapse of a national film industry. In 1972, Turkey was the third-largest film producer in the world, with 300 feature films; at the beginning of the 1990s, fewer than half-a-dozen films were produced. Since then, the Turkish film industry has recovered somewhat; a young generation of filmmakers, developing its films according to its own cultural image and narrative tradition, is establishing itself alongside broad commercial film production for the booming video market.

The shooting star and most important forerunner of the *Cinema Nôvo* was Glauber Rocha (1938–1981). In a manifesto he defined "the aesthetics of hunger" (1965) as distinct from the dominant "aesthetics of imperialism." He justified force as a means of resistance and called for a move toward a violent cinema, at the expense of narrative causality, in stylistically violent and graphic pictures. He viewed his action film *Antonio das Mortes* (1968), in which the cold-blooded killer depicted served as an allegory for the new regime, as an act of "guerilla filmmaking."

The new Latin American cinema

The atmosphere of fundamental change in the 1960s did not stay limited to Europe and North America. In the countries of the Third World, the political struggle for self-determination and against economic exploitation and political repression—the Cuban revolution, the Algerian struggle for independence, the independence movements in Africa and Vietnam—also led to a new revolutionary self-understanding of the artistic community. The Brazilian *Cinema Nôvo* will serve here as an example of the many politically motivated and artistically innovative movements in cinema.

The screens of Latin America had been dominated, since the First World War, by the products of the Hollywood dream factory. Like the European avant-garde filmmakers, the Brazilian directors had trained their eyes and their own powers of expression on the classical Hollywood film and arrived at comparable aesthetic results in the critical debate over its conventions.

In contrast to the works of their European colleagues, however, the films of the young Brazilian directors, however, were much more radical in their criticism and political stances. They were politically engaged citizens of a developing country, ascribing to art a function of serving the struggle for freedom and casting themselves as spokespersons for the oppressed—the ethnic minorities, the farmers, and non-land owning farm-workers. Influenced by the works of the Italian neorealists and the French *Nouvelle Vague*, they adapted stylistic innovations, such as the use of hand cameras or filming in long, planned sequences and combined them with typical Latin American folklore.

The boom in serial films

The rise of the young *auteurs*, artists who both wrote and directed their films, was without a doubt the most exciting and aesthetically successful contribution to the history of film of the 1960s and 1970s. However, although the new wave cinema had certainly attracted its own following, which represented a new cinema-loving public for the art film, it was never cinema for the masses. The general public continued to stream to the glittering productions of Hollywood and its established European and Asian offshoots. Actually, attendance slowed to a trickle since the international crisis of the film industry peaked in the early 1960s. A major decline in the movie industry set in, and film production sank to just one quarter of what it had been in the 1940s.

Such circumstances were hardly conducive to further aesthetic development in commercial cinema. Risks were to be avoided at all costs, so the mainstream cinema turned into a medium

The secret of the success of the James Bond series lies in its equally suspenseful and entertaining mixture of crime, science fiction, and erotic comedy. The hero is cultured and brutal at the same time, a fantastic fighter and irresistible hero of women, who always saves the world from destruction (naturally, at the last second) by an almost equal but mad, evil power while uttering a witty quip. With this successful recipe, the character has survived different lead actors and directors and has inspired numerous imitations and parodies.

The successful Karl May films, which unleashed the series boom in Germany, were the first European productions which dared to enter the domain of the most original of American genres, the western.

of simplemindedness and familiar story lines that had already withstood the test of time, remaining so into the 1970s. The producers, who could make fewer and fewer films because of rising costs, tried to outdo everything that had come before in terms of glamour, elaborateness, and technical effects. Whenever something proved successful, it was immediately turned into a serial. In Germany, for example, very loose but also very popular adaptations of the Karl May's novels and the detective stories of Edgar Wallace dominated the film market, winning the hearts of the public with their endless variations of the same basic motifs and predictable casts of characters.

The most successful film series of the 1960s was a series of spy thrillers involving the British secret agent 007, James Bond, beginning with Terence Young's *Dr. No* (1962), which brought the actor Sean Connery to international fame. It is worth noting that the Bond series was not produced in Hollywood but in London, though it was made—as were 90 percent of all films produced by the British during those years— with American capital.

American film producers found the English capital especially attractive during the 1960s for several reasons. Government financial support for English film productions, London's proximity to the great film markets of Europe, and the high technical standards of British studios contributed to London's status as the film center of the world, a position it held for a decade.

The end of the genre film

The relaxing of the traditional borders between genres, as is evident in the James Bond series, was characteristic of mainstream cinema of the late 1960s and early 1970s. Films seeking to

The clear separation between good and evil in the western classic *Once Upon a Time in the West*, a concession to the American co-producers, was an exception among the so-called "spaghetti westerns."

have the broadest possible public appeal had to offer something for men and women, for young and old, and for people of different cultural backgrounds. The traditional genres could no longer met these criteria.

The later westerns, for example, moved away from the fundamental premise of the genre by critically reflecting on the myth of the good pioneer who was morally strong but also tamed the land with a firm hand. John Ford (1895–1973), the old master of the genre, corrected the portrayal of the evil and blood-thirsty Indian in *Cheyenne Autumn* (1963), and in *The Man Who Shot Liberty Valance* (1961) questioned his own legends of an older, better America.

Only the impartiality/freedom from prejudice of European film producers rejuvenated the western for a brief period, allowing it one last heyday. In the alternative to the pessimistic late American westerns offered by Sergio Corbucci and Sergio Leone, known as "spaghetti westerns," the classical separation of good and evil is entirely discarded and its callous heroes fight and win only for themselves. After standouts including Leone's *A Fistful of Dollars* (1964) and *Once Upon a Time in the West* (1968) and Corbucci's *The Mercenary* (1968), the cynical distancing from the myth of the traditional,

In the 1970s, a new action genre from Hong Kong, the "eastern," got the better of the classic western. It took the Chinese-American actor Bruce Lee only a few films to rise to a cult star of the new films glorifying violence around the martial arts of Kung Fu. Although the film industry of Hong Kong ranked among the strongest in

honorable west lapsed increasingly into irony, as can be seen in Leone's *The Good, The Bad, and the Ugly* (1966), and finally deteriorated into purely entertaining parody in the films starring Bud Spencer and Terence Hill, including *Four Flies on Grey Velvet* (1971), directed by Enzo Barboni Clucher, among many others.

In other genres as well, the traditional repertoire of standard plot lines was subject to transmogrification. For example, in his gory

cinematic spectacle *Dance of the Vampires* (1967), Roman Polanski (b. 1933) allowed evil to ruthlessly conquer good and replaced the mechanics of horror with satirical hyperbole, peopling the film with affectionate comical types. The apotheosis of the mixing of genres and genre

the world in 1972, the year *Fists of Fury* was produced, exclusively the easterns were taken notice of in the West.

parody was reached in 1974 by the hilariously gruesome cult musical, *The Rocky Horror Picture Show* (Jim Sharman, 1974), which gleefully ridiculed elements of vampire and monster films, science fiction spectacles and musicals.

From the dream factory to the nightmare factory

The horror film's degeneration into a weak-plotted, and especially gory, subcategory of zombie and splatter films was only made possible by the demise of the long standing taboos that had regulated the cinema up until the 1970s.

With the decline of the studio system, the American cinema liberalized its strict censorship system, the famous Production Code. The rigid

"Don'ts" which had limited the portrayal of sex and violence under strict rules, proved to be outdated and damaging to business in the battle for the attention and dollars of an increasingly youthful public at a time of general liberalization. The most sought-after new genres were cultish witch and devil films, such as William Friedkin's *The Exorcist* (1973) and Polanski's *Rosemary's Baby* (1967), or the somewhat more realistic disaster movies such as Ronald Neame's *The Poseidon Adventure* (1972) and *The Towering Inferno* by John Guillermin and Irwin Allen (1974).

While Stanley Kubrick (b. 1928) critically examined the growing problem of violence in society in his thoroughly brutal film *A Clockwork Orange*, presenting it as structurally and socially based, the popular occult and disaster films served primarily as

The cinematic adaptation of the theater play *The Rocky Horror Picture Show* (1974) called for entirely new audience behavior. The cult film gave rise to its own "scene," in which the public rediscovered the cinema as a place of experience, attended its favorite film in costumes of the characters, recited their dialogue by heart, threw rice during the wedding scene, and danced in the theater along with the choreography.

As with the portrayal of sexuality, the public was divided in its reaction to violent scenes. In Stanley Kubrick's brutal vision of the future, *Clockwork Orange* (1971), some skeptics saw nothing more than voyeuristic effects while others interpreted the stylized aesthetics of the film as critical distancing from violence.

153

The wave of occult films, which achieved sensational box-office success in 1973 with the shocking *The Exorcist*, presented to its viewers, who were increasingly uncertain amid moral and political crises, "the evil force;" an unexplainable power which forced its way into the lives of ordinary people but could be conquered through the power of familial love and faith.

outlets for coping with anxiety.

Whether its portrayal in film was critical or glorifying, violence would become one of the most important themes of the 1980s and 1990s; the cinema evolved from a dream factory into a nightmare factory. Just as Hollywood had helped its audiences repress their dreary realities during the Depression by offering its endless variations of the American dream, the popular escalation of violence on the screen might be explained by the fact that such frequent portrayal of disaster in the cinema now makes the real world seem comparatively harmless, and thus serves as a release from the increasingly threatening atmosphere of society.

Sexual emancipation

Liberalization in the portrayal of sexuality proved to be as lucrative as the new emphasis on violence. The state-contracted educational film *Helga*, in which the sex expert Oswalt Kolle uninhibitedly fields questions about contraception and childbirth, became a media event in Germany in 1967 and prompted a wave of "schoolgirl reports," a German genre of sex films made under a fairly weak pretense of education.

In other parts of Europe, the United States, and Japan, similar educational films and increasingly explicit sex films were so successful that the step to soft pornography, and finally to hard-core pornography, was a small one. In 1968, Denmark became the first country in the world to legalize pornography. The first hard-core porn film publicly shown in the United States was *Deep Throat* (1972); the owner of the theater where the film premiered was jailed twice during the film's run for pandering pornographic films.

The example of France illustrates how enthusiastically the removal of sex taboos impacted the cinema worldwide: of the 607 new films which were shown in Paris in 1974, the soft porn *Emanuelle* was seen by the most viewers and roundly outmatched other box office successes of the year, such as George Roy Hill's *The Sting* (1973) and *The Exorcist*. Even today, various censorship groups, mostly motivated by concern for protecting youth, over and over have to wrestle with the complicated distinctions among "erotic art films," which frequently revolve around the connection between politics and sexuality; harmless sex films that generally are satisfied with presenting the nude female body in selective color photography; and sexist pornography. Time and again, films that have been celebrated as works of art at international film festivals fall victim to this ongoing uncertainty. This happened in 1975 to Pasolini's controversial *Salo—The 120 Days of Sodom*, which for a short time was removed from video rental shelves in Italy, and Nagisa Oshima's *In the Realm of the Senses*, which was confiscated at the Berlin Festival in 1976 and even in Japan (actually a country with a rich tradition of erotic art) subject to numerous editings, is still banned today in some countries.

Sexuality showed itself as a destructive power in the film *In the Realm of the Senses* (1976) The lover of a young prostitute allows himself, out of sexual obsession, to be strangled and castrated as his partner achieves her climax.

The "Global Village"

The rebellion of the younger generation of the '60s (despite, or even because of, the escalating use of force in the 1970s' confrontations within nations) led in the 1980s to a reconsolidation of traditional relationships of power and possession. In place of the dream of a liberated society emerged a vacuum of values; uncertainty, anxiety about the future, and finally an increase in reactionary tendencies and backward-looking utopias were prevalent. After the arms race between East and West had assumed more and more threatening forms with the building of the neutron bomb and plans to shift atomic weapons into space, even the rapprochement between East and West and the disintegration of the Warsaw Pact at the beginning of the 1990s failed to bring an end to worldwide conflicts. In the crisis-prone hot spots of Africa, South America, and Southeast Asia as well as in new areas in the Gulf and in the Balkans, military confrontations reached a new intensity—also in terms of media representation—as well as a shocking degree of brutality comparable to the that of the Holocaust.

Insecurity was bolstered by the persistent economic crisis in the East and West — growing poverty, unemployment, and the societal tensions attendant to them. The horrible reports of nuclear accidents, environmental disasters, deaths of forests, and worldwide climactic changes contributed their share and made eminently clear that unlimited economic growth and blind belief in progress were not sufficient to secure the future of humankind.

These multi-faceted uncertainties may have contributed to a societal trend, clearly observable at least in the Western world: the phenomenon of cocooning, the retreat of the yuppies into the family, with children as their focal point. Feminists preached of a new motherhood in the 1980s, and children began to have a considerable impact upon consumer behavior. Neil Postman proclaimed *The Disappearance*

Tim Burton's *Batman* (1988), the hit of 1989, was produced for 85 million dollars and has brought in an estimated 500 million dollars at the box office, 300 million dollars through video distribution, and 18 million dollars from television. There has been additional income from music, the sale of books and comics, and licenses for other merchandise such as T-shirts and Batman figures, which created increased public awareness of the film even before it was released.

of Childhood in an infantile society. In any case, the media discovered children as a theme and also reached out to them as a powerful target group of consumers.

At the same time, the world moved toward becoming a "global village;" supported by the network of information technology, the formerly Communist countries integrated themselves into the capitalist world market, and the geographically specific earmarks of cultural expression found themselves confronted with burgeoning competition in the worldwide marketing of mass multimedia products. These products also found a growing consumer base among intellectuals and cultural trendsetters. In the arts, the trivial and the profane experienced a renewed valuation through pop culture. The old dichotomy between high and low culture receded, because the self-centered, career- and consumer-oriented yuppies sought relaxation, rather than education or edification, from culture.

The wonderful new world of media

The beginning of the 1980s marked the inception of the information age. The microcomputer revolution will perhaps one day go down in history as the most significant event of the latter 20th century. But it was only one of several decisive steps toward a society totally dominated by media. In the 1980s, there was a rapid expansion of the video market and of cable and satellite television, which provided the technical basis for the ever-increasing number of private and commercial television broadcasters.

The modern cinema film has to assert itself today in an entirely transformed media landscape, where it is no longer the leading product, but has become one of the entertainment industry's many different products, which serve different audiences and effectively complement one another. The initial success of a feature film in the cinema is decisive in determining the success of its marketing in television and video. In the process, video stores, which have

long since gone beyond storing old lower-end, cheaply produced materials, can become enormously profitable businesses. The profits from video sales of Disney's *Beauty and the Beast* (1991), for example, exceeded the cinema receipts of all previously made films. Despite all the concerns raised initially, the video

Multiplex consumer temples of steel and glass, conceived as entertainment centers, offer "more than cinema" in at least seven theaters (totaling at least 1700 seats) generously equipped with comfortable arena seating, curved mammoth screens, and technical perfection in sound and projections as well as additional leisure activities such as dining and shopping malls.

recorder has, thanks to its widespread use, created a much larger audience for films than would have been possible in the movie theaters, and it has impinged upon the cinema as little as the cinema had upon television. Even the new audiovisual equipment, such as the digital CD-ROM, will surely change the nature of the video store but will not entirely do away with it.

The demand for a continuing stream of new entertainment products has continued to grow in the leisure society; the products are accessible to the most diverse lifestyles in various media. While "amphibian" films were produced for adaptation to various media, each media has developed a specific marketing structure. An entire series of films is produced today for direct-to-video use. The specialization in minority offerings (especially horror and sex films, which are excluded from publicly accessible TV channels and the cinema in order to protect youth) has given the video shops the undeserved reputation of being bastions of smut for adults. Along with television, they have become the main preservers of the cinematic past, because many old films are only available in rental stores.

Television reaches its highest viewing ratings with media-specific formats such as sport and information broadcasts, game and talk shows as well as the addictively consumed daily soap operas. The movies produced for the cinema market are primarily A-pictures made at tremendous cost with budgets exceeding 200 million dollars. The risks for financial backers are minimized as much as possible so that they can be optimally marketed internationally, and

Video

Video technology is a picture-storage process in which the optical signals are divided up into electronic impulses and recorded on magnetic tape, very similar to the recording of sound on tape; like sound recording, the videotape can be copied, replayed, or erased. Video is used today both for film production and as a technique for recording television broadcasts. Experiments were already made in the 1920s with the magnetic storing of pictures, and in the area of television, the first recorder was introduced in 1956 for use as storage and processing equipment. Elaborately-staged music video clips have become a genre in their own right; record producers provide them free of charge to television channels such as MTV, which have specialized in top music programs. Originally purely a means of advertising for music, the especially quick associative montage of the music clips have developed a new video language, whose aesthetics are frequently influenced by a known film director, and in turn have their effect on film production. At the beginning of the 1970s, attempts made to expand video technology beyond its professional studio use to private consumers as well. The over 50 different, mostly incompatible recording processes simultaneously cast upon the market could not gain a foothold, and by the middle of the 1970s, Japanese and European electronics firms such as Philips and Sony set off a home recorder boom with new standards and inexpensive equipment. For a long time, no one could have conceived of a business involving used cassettes; the film companies feared inroads at the box office. The video trade only got into full swing at the end of the 1970s when a failed Hollywood actor placed a small ad in the *Los Angeles Times*, in which he offered to rent films in his personal possession. At first, primarily third class films came to the rental market, but recently the majority of revenues are made with films that began successfully in the movie theaters. In the meantime, there are video stores on every street corner, but the video business is already in decline because the market for the purchase of video cassettes is booming. Cheap tapes can be found today right next to the supermarket checkout counter.

the films therefore have to be culturally compatible and highly standardized. The construction of multiplex theaters with larger, technically better-equipped cinemas built into shopping malls and offering a modern gastronomic experience has made the visit to the cinema a point of interest in a new form of entertainment culture. This strategy has led to considerable audience growth among the over thirty-year-old demographic group, whose attendance had been dwindling since the 1970s.

The new British television-film miracle

That the harsh competition between film industry and television could finally lead to peaceful coexistence is a direct result of the restructuring of the media market. Cinema, television, and video films, along with sound recorders, CD-ROMs, and software, are no longer produced by media-specific firms in competition with one another, but side-by-side in the same factories belonging to several large media conglomerates. Outside of the commercial interests, the cooperation between television broadcasters and producers of cinema films has proven to be artistically fruitful. The new German film of the 1970s, for example, owes a large part of its success to the financial support of public broadcasters. In the 1980s, while the European film languished, independent British producers surprised the world with stylistically very different films of high artistic quality, which were critical of society and had been commissioned by television networks.

The British film industry actually found itself in one of its most difficult crises at the end of the 1970s, brought about on the one hand by the retreat of American investors, which had for a short time made London into a world center for film, and on the other hand by decreasing audiences as a result of the rise of television. Like no other country, England had been continually a colony of Hollywood, which, apart from

Richard Attenborough's (b. 1923) *Gandhi* is a monumental biographical epic along the lines of the Hollywood classics, with an offering of the best British actors and 350,000 extras. It is also an intelligent film which pleads for a humanistic world view at a time when taking a political stance in the cinema was the exception. The film was awarded eight Oscars.

the brief movements of the British Documentary Film school in the 1940s and of the Free Cinema of the 1960s, could barely create its own profile. Perhaps the lack of American investors prompted the readiness to experiment and the critical stance against English society of the Thatcher era, which was marked by social Darwinism and a

compassionless, overachieving mentality. Many directors of the New British Cinema walked the line between different artistic genres, which explains the special formal structure of their films as well as the clear influence of the graphic arts, literature, and modern theater.

"The British are coming!" scriptwriter Colin Wellman proudly proclaimed at the Academy Awards in 1981 when he was recognized, along with director Hugh Hudson, for *Chariots of Fire* (1980). The film tells the true story of two British medal winners at the Olympic Games in 1924.

The rejuvenation of quality British films had already been proclaimed with the multiple Oscar awards for Hugh Hudson's *Chariots of Fire* (1980) and Richard Attenborough's *Gandhi* (1982). But the revitalization of the British cinema would not have been possible without the arrival of television's Channel 4 in 1980—a result of one of the last laws enacted by the labor government—which was not supposed to produce its own material, but commission work within Great Britain. The nationwide broadcast specialized in a type of "television for the average citizen" in which ethnic minorities and other socially disadvantaged groups had their say.

The entry into feature film production, whereby the television channel commissioned exclusively independent producers, was encouraged by a law which freed investment in feature films from taxes during the first year, and by financial assistance from the British Film Institute. After the first international successes among the approximately 12 films produced annually for Channel 4 (which were, however, first seen in the cinema), other British broadcasters began to award contracts to independent British producers.

The directors of the New British Cinema have recognized that our society no longer consists of "normal average citizens," but of outsiders. The new, everyday heroes are, for example, a young Pakistani and an unemployed Englishman

who, in protest against the racism and prejudice of an overachieving society, turn a dead-beat laundromat into a flourishing business and in the process fall in love with one another. *My Beautiful Laundrette*, a work commissioned by Channel 4, was the 1985 surprise success of director Stephen Frears (b. 1941), who began his career in the theater.

Society consists of outsiders

The artistic results were of course less homogeneous than the slogan "New British Cinema" would lead one to believe. Compared to Italian neorealism, the French *Nouvelle Vague*, or the New German Film, the New British Cinema lacked unifying aesthetic cinematic elements, as well as the typical revolutionary spirit of a new group of artists. Alongside sweeping epics, such as Roland Joffé's *The Mission* (1986) and *A Passage to India* (1984) by the Hollywood returnee David Lean, which splendidly linked the American successful formula with British quality, stood a series of lower-class films. In good Anglo-Saxon tradition, these films included stories about the unemployed, street people, prostitutes, and gay small businessmen for the screen. From Stephen Frear's criticism of racism in *My Beautiful Laundrette* (1985) to Danny Boyle's shocking junkie portrait *Trainspotting* (1995), there is a common theme of engagement for societal outsiders.

The socially critical movies of the New British Cinema document the filmmakers' recognition of the fact that every segment of society is important, and that there is therefore no longer just one but several realities. With their defense of societal fringe groups, the filmmakers protested against the ruling Thatcher government's version of justice, against the prevailing of the majority for conformity and sought to acknowledge the heterogeneity of an increasingly multi-cultural society.

In comparison with these often comic socio-critical studies, James Ivory's romantic filmings of literary works (*A Room With a View*, 1987) seem highly stylized. The films of the American-born Ivory and his American producer Ismail Merchant are among the most internationally successful efforts of the New British Cinema, perhaps because they reconstruct what is stereotypically British even better than the

British themselves: psychologically perceptive dramas set among the upper class, presented in lavish photography of English landscape and architecture.

Innovative language, experimental aesthetics, and the breaking of taboos characterize the films of the artists Derek Jarman (1942–1994) and Peter Greenaway (b. 1942). Jarman's recurring theme is the search for homosexual identity. In *Caravaggio* (1986) and *Edward II* (1991), he chose the format of historical subject matter, while in his last film, *Blue* (1993), he confronted his audience with his own AIDS. His background as a painter and set designer led him to develop a refreshing approach to creating scenery, which always demanded active involvement on the part of the viewers. For over 80 minutes, *Blue* shows nothing but a blue backdrop while passages gleaned from Jarman's diaries are read from off-screen.

Like Jarman, the eccentric Peter Greenaway began as an experimental filmmaker, but with his first feature film *The Draughtsman's Contract* (1982) achieved international success early in his career. His films are complex puzzles full of quotes from Western intellectual tradition (*Prospero's Books*, 1991) and shocked his audiences with bizarre stories around themes such as impotence, crime, and cannibalism (*The Cook, the Thief, His Wife, and Her Lover*, 1989).

In *Caravaggio*, Derek Jarman tells the story of a homosexual painter who does not want to conform to societal norms. The film is at the same time a reflection on the interrelationship between art and eroticism.

Peter Greenaway narrated his films, as did only few directors of the 1980s, in opulent pictures and colors. In the stylization of his settings, he moves toward visual art, creating his scenes with the compositional means of the theater. His stories, often presented in puzzling sequences of pictures, break with the strongest societal taboos and are therefore heavily debated by the public and the critics. Scene from *The Cook, the Thief, His Wife, and Her Lover* (1989).

The new boom of the cinema

The international media market today is controlled by a few worldwide entertainment conglomerates from the United States, Japan, Germany, and Australia who, of course, primarily invest their money in the production of films in Hollywood's dream factory. While film is promoted as an art form in the European countries, right from the beginning Americans have engaged in production for the purpose of

maximizing profits and strove relentlessly, even during the worst crisis of the industry in the 1960s and 1970s, to adapt their films to changing market requirements and to develop new sales markets.

Thus the films of Hollywood, or more accurately those of a rejuvenated New Hollywood, have represented the main attraction for the slowly returning world cinema audience since the middle of the 1970s. American film producers today enjoy an 80 percent share of the world market and have been reporting new sales records almost yearly since 1985. An example from the 1990s: Steven Spielberg's *Jurassic Park* (1993) became the most lucrative film of all time, with a record revenue of 50.16 million dollars, on its first weekend. It was dethroned quickly in 1996 by Brian de Palma's *Mission: Impossible* (74.13 million dollars), until Spielberg was able to assert himself again in 1997 with *Jurassic Park's* sequel, *The Lost World* (over 100 million dollars). Only those able to implement Hollywood's formula for success can keep pace, and even then the comparatively strong film industries of Hong Kong, India, and Europe have only a marginal impact on the world market.

The success of a film can be predicted with as little certainty as the weather. But spectacular financial failures have always existed alongside Hollywood's giant hits. Michael Cimino's *Heaven's Gate* brought in only 1.5 million dollars against the production costs of 44 million, and actor/producer Kevin Costner literally took a dive with the most expensive film project up to that time, his 170 million dollar *Water World*, in 1994.

New Hollywood in the 1970s: think young

The renewal of Hollywood was brought about by small independent producers after the decline of the great studios and the deep aesthetic crisis of the "Sad Sixties." While the old Hollywood dug its own grave by disregarding the costs of increasingly superficial musicals and historical drivel, which fewer and fewer people wanted to see, the independents soon recognized that contemporary, up-to-date themes were necessary amid the new mood of the late 1960s. Roger Corman (b. 1926), producer and director, belongs to a group of filmmakers who first reached only an insider public with their well-directed, low-budget productions, horror films, teenage comedies, and drug and motorcycle films.

Easy Rider clearly struck a nerve of the day: underscored with lively rock-and-roll music, the film celebrates the hippie generation's dream od freedom in its passing pictures of a staggering landscape. However, the motorcycle knights of the open road are outsiders who encounter only narrow-mindedness, cynicism, and violence on their search for the original American dream of freedom and tolerance. Their dream trip becomes a nightmare and ends in their senseless death on the road.

Like in the very early years of the film industry, Bob Rafelson, Jack Nicholson, Peter Fonda, and Dennis Hopper worked alternately as directors, producers, and actors in these films.

With *Easy Rider*, which Hopper directed, Fonda produced, and both acted in along with Nicholson, the genre of the Road Movie was promoted to worldwide popularity in 1969. The surprising success of the film, which brought in over 50 million dollars compared to its production costs of 400,000 dollars, paved the way for other outsiders to take part in big business and unleashed a wave of imitations. Other outstanding independent productions included Robert Altman's satire of war *M*A*S*H* (1969), Sidney Lumet's police film *Serpico* (1973), and David Lynch's *Eraserhead* (1977). Russ Meyer created a humorously critical mixture of sex and action films (among them *Super Vixens*, 1975). John Cassavetes' off-Hollywood productions are characterized by their marvelous acting, original cinematic language, and a new cinematic look at gender roles. His body of work is difficult to categorize, but has had great impact on the next generation of directors.

The Hollywood "Majors" began to pay greater attention to these outsiders from the beginning of the 1970s and started to absorb themes, formal

Jack Nicholson (b. 1937) is one of the first artists of the New Hollywood. He received his first Oscar for the leading role in Miloš Forman's *One Flew Over the Cuckoo's Nest* (1975), a parable about the conflict between individuality and conformity, which takes a mental institution as the symbol for all of American society.

In its search for themes and material which concerned the present-day audience, New Hollywood came upon the Vietnam War. A whole wave of films was initiated with Michael Cimino's *The Deerhunter* (1978), including Francis Ford Coppola's *Apocalypse Now* (1976–1979), the *Rambo* series (1982–1987) with the main actor and film script author Sylvester Stallone, and Kubrick's *Full Metal Jacket* (1987). Again

and again the approach wavers between revulsion at one's own brutality and the attempts to come to terms with the United States' first great military defeat. Scene from Oliver Stone's impressive anti-war film, *Platoon* (1986).

innovations, and some of the stars of the alternative cinema. Young filmmakers like Robert Altman, Peter Bogdanovich, Francis Ford Coppola and Martin Scorsese suddenly got their chance. With stories about homosexuality and racism, sexual problems, and the generational conflict, they aimed—with an eye toward the changing structure of their audience—at young viewers.

However, anyone wanting to be successful in Hollywood also had to adapt to the demands of the dream factory. The strong-willed artist John Cassavetes, for example, swore never again to direct for a studio after having unpleasant experiences with contract work for Hollywood. Most of his later films were made outside Hollywood, and the excellent actor put all of the money he earned from roles in successful films such as *Rosemary's Baby* (1967) into his own projects. Director-artists like Cassavetes created a new regard for the American cinema against the background of a fundamentally changing conception of art. From that point on, even films of the American entertainment and genre cinema were taken seriously by the popular press, as was previously the case only with the theater or literature.

The victory march of the brat pack

By contrast, the "movie brats," as the Americans called their young generation of directors in the late 1970s and early 1980s, had the very best qualifications for walking the thin line between the commercial demands of Hollywood and individual artistic demands. The typical movie brat was born in 1940 or later, had already learned his craft at a film academy, and regarded the European literary cinema as highly as the beloved Hollywood classics.

Making connection to the great traditions of the dream factory is one of the main trends that can be identified in the New Hollywood of the 1980s. The old masters have repeatedly been paid homage by directors such as Francis Ford Coppola, George

Lucas, Steven Spielberg, Martin Scorsese, Brian de Palma, John Carpenter, and Mel Brooks, in works in which they have drawn on the classics or even remade the great films, in passionate or ironically endearing tributes. The aesthetic of the New Hollywood is a postmodern one of quotation.

John Carpenter filmed a pessimistic remake of Howard Hawks' *The Thing* in 1982 which he effectively used to showcase the possibilities of new animation techniques; in 1976, he updated the conflict in his western classic *Rio Bravo* to a modern-day big city western in *Assault on Precinct 13*. Brian de Palma paid homage to the genre master in 1983 with a dark and violent new filming of the famous gangster classic, *Scarface* with Al Pacino in the leading role. He became famous with his Hitchcock reminiscences *Obsession* (1976), a variation on *Vertigo*, and the thriller *Dressed to Kill* (1980), which draws upon the masterpiece *Psycho*.

But the movie brats not only recreated individual films of their great Hollywood masters, they also retrained their focus on the classical genre cinema, which had died out in the 1960s. This return to proven models laid the foundation for the re-emergence of Hollywood. The risks of genre productions can be calculated: the formula is familiar, they are easy to produce, and they can be sold as standardized mass products to a broad public throughout the world.

Three legendary films of the 1970s illustrate how Hollywood was taken over by the equally tradition-minded and innovative movie brats. In 1971 Francis Ford Coppola (b. 1939) was successful with *The Godfather*, a masterwork of the gangster film, which perfectly joined a socially critical perspective with gripping entertainment and overshadowed all previous Hollywood box office successes, including *Gone with the Wind* (1939) and *Doctor Zhivago* (1965), the uncontested blockbusters of the past. After a

Not all genres were revived in New Hollywood: westerns, crime films, family melodramas, and gangster films migrated to television— mostly in serial form. Most successful were science fiction, adventure films, the gory horror films. John Carpenter set new standards in 1978 with *Halloween* in terms of both the degree of brutality and the formal quality of the genre.

In part, *The Godfather* owes its success to the splendid acting of one older Hollywood star and one younger one: Marlon Brando (right) and Al Pacino (left).

long period of wasting away, the film industry seemed to have entered a new age, for in 1974 the newcomer Steven Spielberg (b. 1947) announced his arrival with the thriller *Jaws*, which, in the tradition of Hitchcock's *The Birds*, conjured up fear as exploited nature avenges itself on people for destroying the environment. Spielberg's film was only able to retain first-place as the top-grossing movie of all time for three years before he was replaced by George Lucas' (b. 1944) *Star Wars* (1977), which along with Kubrick's *2001: A Space Odyssey* (1965–1968), introduced the renaissance of the science fiction genre.

Blockbusters follow

The box office hits of the 1970s made Coppola, Lucas, and Spielberg superstars in Hollywood's director's scene, where they continue to set the tone for the enormous film business until today. Their debut successes represent everything that New Hollywood embodies. *The Godfather*, *Jaws*, and *Star Wars* were genre productions created according to the successful patterns of traditional Hollywood cinema and, at the same time, set new standards with the introduction of modern animation technology and the quality of their scripts. All three films were blockbusters geared for commercial success, which covered their production costs within a few weeks.

Star Wars catapulted the film industry to a new economic dimension. Its marketing was not limited to income at the box office; the fantasy/science fiction film provided the young video trade with its first best-seller and aimed to achieve equally high returns from the sale of fan paraphernalia. No wonder the film industry attempted to exploit such goldmines for a second and even a third time with sequels. Of course, sequels seldom achieve the quality of the original film, but box office success is nevertheless guaranteed. The profitable follow-up films of *The Godfather*, *Jaws*, and *Star Wars* have led to the fact that sequels are already planned when an original (anticipated) blockbuster is being produced. Thus, in *Halloween* (1978), Carpenter had the apparent corpse of the insane murderer inexplicably disappear, a first-class horror effect that left open the option for continuation. By 1990, Michael Myers had returned five times to the scene of his atrocities to continue his bloody handiwork. The same thing was true of Sylvester Stallone's muscular fighter *Rocky*, who was also sent into the boxing ring five times, while *Superman* was allowed to return only four times to combat the arch-fiend Lex Luthor.

The continued resurrection of *Alien* (1979), which haunted movie theaters for the fourth time in 1997, shows that a film topic can still be good for a sequel many years after its first filming. George Lucas predicted this trend as early as 1977: In a contract with Twentieth Century Fox, he sold the distribution rights for *Star Wars* for less than it was worth and negotiated in its place sole ownership of rights to possible sequels. Inspired by the continuing success of the *Star Wars* trilogy, he is now at work on a prequel, which recounts the history prior to the first installment.

Since the 1970s, the use of the most spectacular special effects has become more and more important for the box office success of a film. The manufacturing and servicing of the three hydraulically animated polyurethane monsters that alternately embodied the monster in *Jaws* is said to have devoured over three million dollars — a third of the entire production cost of the film.

169

May the force be with you

As a fairy-tale mixture of everything that Hollywood makes so wonderfully colorful and successful, *Star Wars* fascinated a public that today is spoiled by special effects. In 1997, Lucas cast a new version of the trilogy onto the market with the aid of improved digital technology in sound and picture, attracting 25 million Americans to the theater within several weeks.

Personal union of direction and production

The trendsetters Coppola, Lucas, and Spielberg exemplify a further phenomenon of the New Hollywood. While in the old studio system those responsible for the financing increasingly limited the influence of the artists and even barred them from making the final cut, this development has been reversed in the New Hollywood. The artists, first the star directors and then in their wake more and more movie stars, seized control again and assumed financial responsibility for their projects as well. With the help of the enormous income from the merchandising of Star Wars products, George Lucas fulfilled a dream and founded his own film empire under the name Lucasfilm Ltd. For the sequels *The Empire Strikes Back* (1979) and *The Return of the Jedi* (1982), he wrote only the script and subsequently dedicated himself to the further development of special effects technology. Before him, his mentor Francis Ford Coppola had already attempted to oppose the firmly established power structure of the Hollywood majors by founding an alternative studio, Zoetrope, albeit less successfully. Steven Spielberg made the jump from outstanding director to tycoon of the film business and now rivals Microsoft's Bill Gates for the position of wealthiest American. Like no one else, he has influenced everyday American culture with his own work as director and producer at his Spielberg Factory.

In his 1991 Christmas television special, Bob Hope asked the 11- year-old Macaulay Culkin about the upcoming premiere of the sequel to his box office smash, *Home Alone* (1990), "How could your parents in the movie leave you 'home alone' a second time?" To which the best-paid child star in the world responded, "Because the studio racked up 500 million dollars the first-time!" (quoted in The New Guinness Book of Film)

The youngest tycoon

The success story of Hollywood's wunderkind began in television, where Spielberg drew attention to himself as the 22-year-old director of hit series like *Columbo*. He was more than able to make up for the flops of his first movie *Sugarland Express* (1974) and his fourth work *1941* (1979), with box office smashes *Jaws* and the *Indiana Jones* series, completed by Lucasfilm (*Raiders of the Lost Ark*, 1980; *Indiana Jones and the Temple of Doom*, 1983; *Indiana Jones—the Last Crusade*, 1988).

In his work, Spielberg paid homage over and over again to great Hollywood cinema and demonstrated his extraordinary craftsmanship in all genres of the New Hollywood: *Jaws* (1974) is a gripping horror film, the *Indiana Jones* series offers suspenseful action adventure, *Close Encounters of the Third Kind* (1977) and *E. T. the Extraterrestrial* (1982) are splendid examples of the fantasy science fiction wave of the 1980s in the best Disney tradition. With his dinosaur thrillers about inhabitants of *Jurassic Park* (1993 and 1996), Spielberg proved once again that his perfectly crafted mixtures of classical thriller plot, the accompanying dramatic suspense, and the newest sensations from the special effects kitchens of computer animators lead to certain box office success.

Steven Spielberg has always been forward-looking in his film career, whether it's a question of anticipating trends and changes in Hollywood or directly implementing them. Following his first production company, Amblin, Spielberg founded a second studio in 1994 named DreamWorks, which does not aim to create films for mass-production, but rather as serious and socially conscious works. At the same time he brought together a television department, a music label, and a software division under one roof.

In his work, Spielberg relies not only on effects and suspense, but also on the emotions of the audience. Again and again, it is the childlike heroes of his films who remind the adults in the audience of the dream of a more peaceful, better world. *The Color Purple* (1986), *Empire of the Sun* (1987) and *Schindler's List* (1993) are attempts to demonstrate his capacities as a cinematic artist with the filming of serious literature.

On a research mission, an extraterrestrial spaceship apparently leaves the endearing E. T. behind on earth. Little Eliott befriends the shy extraterrestrial and protects him from the reckless research efforts of the grownups. In the end, the ten year-old helps the homesick being return home. The suspenseful and gently comic gem of the new family cinema topped the all-time best-seller list for ten years and, interestingly, was not outdone until the arrival of a new Spielberg smash in *Jurassic Park*.

Since the beginning of the 1980s, Spielberg has also been engaged as producer. He trained and fostered his protégé Robert Zemeckis, whose blockbusters *Back to the Future I–III* (1985/1989/1990) and *Who Framed Roger Rabbit* (1988), a fascinating combination of feature film and cartoon which clearly bears the signature of the Spielberg Factory; this is true as well of Tobe Hooper's classic horror film *Poltergeist* (1982) and Joe Dante's sinister, gruesome farce *Gremlins* (1983), to mention some of the most well-known.

New Hollywood as *auteur* cinema

The re-emergence of Hollywood rests on a conscious orientation toward marketability: the trend toward making increasingly expensive films continues up to today. In consideration of the targeted world audience, the films must be highly standardized and culturally compatible in order to bring in the greatest revenue. Ironically, Hollywood's products are at the same time increasingly perceived even in America as works of art. The influential *New York Times* suddenly began discussing cinematic premieres with a seriousness previously reserved for the theater, literature, and the fine arts. The growing interest in the development of an American film art encouraged some directors of commercial cinema to work on their personal artistic signatures and to introduce

A popular theme of New Hollywood was the rediscovery of the recent American past in films which play in charmingly reconstructed decor of the '40s and '50s—a symbol that conjures up of the good old days, when people even still went to the movies. Scene from Robert Zemeckis' *Back to the Future*.

innovative cinematic language, as well as challenging themes, into their productions for mass audiences.

One of the most original filmmakers of New Hollywood is Robert Altman (b. 1925). He employs the conventions of the genre film in order to in some respects turn them on their head, and therefore against the basic ideological foundations of America. *McCabe and Mrs. Miller* (1971) is an anti-western,

Melancholic comedies are the specialty of the independent director Jim Jarmusch, who on the edge of the mainstream, profited from the general upturn of the cinema in the 1980s. *Down by Law* (1986), a rogues' tale of a trio of prison escapees who learn to appreciate and be considerate of one another on their way through Louisiana, immediately gained cult status.

M*A*S*H (1969) a wicked war film parody, while the backstage satire *The Player* (1992) takes aim at Hollywood itself, and criticizes the content as well as the form of the dream factory's products. Altman's films continue to fascinate with their unusual use of technical sound effects. Bits of dialogue from simultaneously occurring conversations overlap, and music and voices from off-camera join together apparently disconnected pictures and narrative strands. With his abrupt cuts and constant changing of camera perspective, he created his own idiosyncratic visual language that fragments reality into the different points of view of disparate individuals. For example his masterpiece, *Nashville* (1974), follows the paths of 24 people over the course of a weekend in brief episodes as they move about at the election party of a presidential candidate.

The demythologized confrontation with the American dream characterizes the work of Martin Scorsese (b. 1942). His films show unadorned pictures of America in detailed milieu studies. His heroes, often portrayed by the outstanding actor Robert de Niro, are outsiders who seek to liberate themselves from the social structures of the Mafia and the rigid Catholicism of their surroundings with extreme brutality. Thus a psychologically twisted bourgeois unleashes a bloodbath in his fight for a purer America in *Taxi Driver* (1975).

Director Robert Altman, during the filming of *Short Cuts* (1993), a kaleidoscope of episodes from the life of 22 Californian couples. He succeeded in creating a disturbing portrait of a society in which true feelings are as rare as responsibility, intimacy, and shame.

While other movie brats rely heavily upon high-tech and special effects in their striving for innovative cinematic expression, Scorsese makes an impact with his dynamic camera movement, whose rhythm develops in close connection with the soundtrack. His cinematic signature mixes stylized forms of the classical genre film with realistic, autobiographically inspired pictures of modern-day big city life. Scorsese's career, consistently accompanied by the highest critical praise, reflects the difficulties of an American author-filmmaker caught between necessary concessions to Hollywood and his own artistic ambition. In order to be able to realize the long-planned projects most important to him, such as the Kafkaesque nightmare of a yuppie, *After Hours* (1985), he continued to agree to make popular, mainstream films such as *The Color of Money* (1986) and *Cape Fear* (1991).

Distinctive among the work of American author filmmakers are the comedies and plays of Woody Allen (b. 1935). Unlike most other American filmmakers, the multi-talented Allen enjoys unusual freedom in his collaborations with the large Hollywood studios (first United Artists, then Orion):

The author and director controls every phase of the production from script to casting to the final cut. While his early slapstick comedies sometimes reveal the silliness of the former TV joke writer, since the end of the 1970s Allen has oriented himself more and more toward his European models Fellini and Bergman and filmed perceptive mixtures of biting satire and subtle psychodrama. In *Annie Hall* (1977), he brought a new comic type to the screen, whom Allen played himself—as with almost all the main roles of his films—and continued to develop in *Manhattan* (1978) and on through *Deconstructing Harry* (1997). With his portrayal of psychological conflicts besetting hypersensitive and complex-ridden Jewish intellectuals, the most successful comedian in America became the chronicler of the neuroses of our times. Forays into serious drama (*Interiors*, 1978), melodrama (*The Purple Rose of Cairo*, 1984) and recently even into the musical (*Everybody Says: I Love You*, 1996) reveal the broad spectrum of a film artist who is as much indebted to the classical Hollywood film as to the European art film.

The work of Spike Lee (b. 1956), the only African American filmmaker who was able to establish himself in Hollywood during the 1980s, represents an extremely successful combination of political involvement and commercial successful in film. Following *She's Gotta Have It* (1986), a romantic comedy which was produced by an exclusively African American ensemble and staff, Lee's films continue to revolve around racial conflicts in the

In *Raging Bull* (1979), Scorsese dismantled the American dream by allowing the world boxing champ to wind up as a honky tonk entertainer. The biography of the self-destructive, violent middle-weight LaMotta was viewed as one of the best films of New Hollywood by many critics.

Annie Hall is the first in a series of films in which Woody Allen deals humorously with the theme of failed love amid the conditions of a modern day big city. Speech directly aimed at the audience, subtitles which disclosed what was really happening, and the skillfully inserted use of documentary techniques and narration in flashbacks made this a sensitive satire and *auteur* film in the European mold. As a protest against Hollywood, Woody Allen did not accept his first Oscars (director, film script, best film).

present day (*Do the Right Thing*, 1988) and the recent past *Malcolm X* (1992).

Cinema in the 1990s

After a history of now over 100 years, the oft-predicted end of the cinema, or even of film itself, is hardly to be expected. The medium has overcome economic crises as well as aesthetic stagnation and technical revolutions. As a whole, the essence of cinematography is still determined by the logic of the business and not by artistic experiment. In an environment of ever-fluctuating consumer mentality and structuring of leisure time, culture takes on a societal function that aims less at education or even critical discussion than on relieving

Quentin Tarantino received the Golden Palm of Cannes in 1994 for his gory, comic thriller *Pulp Fiction*.

stress and offering relaxation to counterbalance the extreme demands of our society. In the course of this development, but also in reaction to the higher standards of a public which now has long years of experience with and exposure to film and television, and demands more from its entertainment, commercial mainstream cinema and artistically ambitious *auteur* films have clearly moved closer together. Cinema lovers enjoyed David Lynch's postmodern road movie *Wild at Heart* (1990) and Quentin Tarantino's *Pulp Fiction* (1993), a mixture of scurrilous farce and brutal action film, while the success of Ang Lee's filming of Jane Austen's *Sense and Sensibility* (1995) made this sensitive writer from the early 19th-century accessible to a broad section of today's public, while Steven Spielberg moved the world deeply with a three-hour black and white film about the Holocaust (*Schindler's List*, 1993).

Due to the worldwide trend to stick even more closely to Hollywood's recipes for success, European and American entertainment products and art films can hardly be differentiated from one another. Countless remakes of successful European films—which have to be produced anew because the American public will not accept dubbing—demonstrate how unproblematically modern European cinema has entered the American mainstream.

The age of computer animation

A hundred years ago, film offered something that had never existed before: moving pictures of reality. Today, film can realistically portray things that cannot exist in reality. The images of resurrected dinosaurs in *Jurassic Park* and *The Lost World* (1993/1996) seem deceptively lifelike; the special effects that allow *Terminator 2*, a murderous, futuristic robot, to pass through walls without a scratch and be transformed into every imaginable human and inorganic form are truly astonishing.

The computer animation for *Jurassic Park* was created by the company Industrial Light & Magic, which was founded in 1975 by George Lucas in order to produce the special effects for *Star Wars*. ILM is the market leader and has been involved in almost all of the important block-busters of the 1990s.

Following the aesthetic upheaval of the 1970s and the restructuring that accompanied the economic upswing of the 1980s, the cinematic innovations of the 1990s are primarily of a technical nature. Just like they were a hundred years ago, people are again drawn to the cinema by the promise of seeing something that never has been seen before. *Terminator 2—Judgment Day*, a film by James Cameron, cashed in on this premise in 1990. The sequel belongs to today's most popular genre, the adventure action thriller, which combines romantic motifs with science fiction and suspense. This combination gives the film industry ample opportunity to show off the fast-paced progress of the special effects industry. The special effects used in *Terminator 2*, at a cost of 17 million dollars,

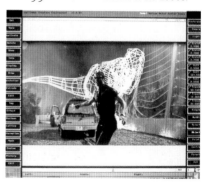

Computer technology makes it possible to digitally alter even the very smallest part of a face. The effects used to meld real and animated film in Charles Russell's *The Mask* (1994) originate from the specialists of ILM.

devoured a fifth of the production costs, which made it clear that anyone wanting to achieve record receipts in the future could not overlook the new technology in computer animation. This is substantiated by a glance at the most commercially successful films of the 1990s, from Tim Burton's fairy tale *Batman Returns* (1991) and Robert Zemeckis' impish, comic story *Forrest Gump* (1993) to Roland Emmerich's apocalyptic science fiction outing *Independence Day* (1995) and the two *Jurassic Park* films.

The most spectacular of the effects in *Terminator 2* are the literally flowing transformations of the malevolent liquid metal Cyborg. Before the viewers' disbelieving eyes and without change of camera, it passes through prison bars, re-emerges from a linoleum floor, assumes the form of a uniformed security guard, and regenerates itself again after apparently total destruction. This technique, which is much more convincing than conventional fades, is called morphing or shape shifting. It is not created with a camera, but calculated and generated on the computer. The beginning and end points of the transformation are filmed conventionally, and the computer then calculates the transformation phases from this data. For the effects in *Terminator 2*, however, insert cuts of handmade models were still used, which lent the image of the different transformation stages brilliance and focus. It is only the real film sequences that create the impression of a perfect shape shifting.

The particular achievement of mask creators and model builders, as well as of the computer animation specialists, lies in the imperceptible integration of the different special effect techniques. Computer animation is not only employed for spectacular effects, but has also become a part of everyday postproduction, the reworking of raw film after filming. Generally, films are still made in the traditional way with film or video material and then edited and enhanced with the special effects.

Special effects are currently produced by many varied techniques. Originally, *Jurassic Park* was supposed to be filmed primarily with conventionally-animated, original-sized dinosaur models. The introduction of digital techniques was only planned for one scene in which a herd of the great beasts were supposed to run over a hill. The animation proved to be so deceptively genuine that Spielberg combined more and more computer pictures with original filmed scenes. Furthermore, many action scenes which were supposed to be filmed with the animated dinosaur models were choreographed in advance on computer. *Toy Story*, the 1995 release that tells the tale of the rivalry between two toy figures for the favor of the the boy they belong to, was the first adventure to be completely generated on computer.

An example of the possibilities of digital composing: Tom Hanks, alias Forrest Gump, meets John F. Kennedy.

With *Forrest Gump*, Zemeckis drew attention to a further astonishing possibility of computer technology. The title hero meets the real John F. Kennedy in one scene. For this effect, bluescreen-shots of Tom Hanks were scanned into documentary film shots. In order to put the words of the film into the mouth of the president, his lip movements were altered by computer manipulation following the patterns of an actor's mouth. Whether this advance will soon lead to further scanning of actors in digital studios is now just a question of time. It is theoretically already possible to create a new film with Marlene Dietrich or Clark Gable through the combination of pictures of live actors and information on deceased actors scanned from old films.

The making of *Toy Story* (director: John Lasseter, 1995) took four years.

With these innovations and all those that will inevitably follow, the potential of the dream factory is boundless.

Brief Overview of the History of Film

Brief overview of the history of film

1893 Edison demonstrates the first short, continuous film strips in his Kinetoscope.

November 1, 1895 The brothers Skladanowsky present the first public "living pictures" in a Berlin variety theater.

December 28, 1895 The brothers Lumière offer the first public showing of film with their *Cinématographe*, which becomes the prototype of cinema technology. The first program contained several variety numbers along with familiar scenes of everyday life.

1896 Establishment of the Pathé Frères film company, which grows to be the world market leader within four years.

1897 The illusionist Georges Méliès opens a film studio in Paris in which he invents the first special effects, the stop trick and double lighting.

1899 The first permanent "cinema shop" is opened in Berlin. Nickelodeons spread throughout the United States, in which movies are shown around the clock for a nickel. The cinema establishes itself as entertainment for the lower classes.

Around 1900 The directors of the school of Brighton use changes of scene and cuts for the first time as directing techniques.

1903 Oskar Messter introduces the first "sound pictures" in Berlin, in which he coordinates the film projector with a gramophone; Edwin S. Porter presents one of the first westerns in the history of film, *The Great Train Robbery*, and creates numerous impulses with his tension-filled directing.

1907 The Lafitte brothers found the *Compagnie des Films d'art* with the intention of producing films of an artistic nature.

1908 In Italy production of monumental historical films begins with *The Last Days of Pompeii*.

1910 The Danish director Urban Gad films *The Abyss*, one of the first feature-length films with the new star Asta Nielsen in the leading role.

1911 In Hollywood, the first film studio is set up.

1912 Mack Sennett starts production of slapstick comedies.

1915 David W. Griffith makes the first American monumental film with *Birth of a Nation* and sets the standards for the development of cinematic art with his advanced montage techniques.

1916 *The Gulf Between* is the first color film to be made using the two strip Technicolor process.

1919 With *The Cabinet of Dr. Caligari*, the short blossoming of expressionistic film begins in Germany. The specific set and lighting style of the film went down in film history as "Caligarism" and influenced genres such as the horror film and the *film noir*.

1920 The German pioneer of special effects, Erich Schüfftan, develops a trick process with mirrors to combine real objects and persons with models; Charles Chaplin films his first full-length film featuring the little tramp character, *The Kid*.

1921 Murnau's *Nosferatu* establishes the genre of the vampire film.

1922 Robert J. Flaherty's *Nanook of the North* becomes the model for feature-length documentary films; a film with integrated light and soundtrack is shown in Berlin for the first time.

Around 1923 The modern saucy "flapper girls" establish themselves as a new type of female star; Rudolph Valentino becomes the first male sex symbol.

1924 Founding of Warner Brothers and MGM

1925 Sergei Eisenstein revolutionizes the art of film montage in *Potemkin*.

1926 The era of the great movie palaces, begun in the United States, also arrives in Germany; in Berlin a cinema opens with 1600 seats.

1927 After the success of Warner Brothers' *The Jazz Singer*, the first sound film in which speech is also used, all the studios switch over to sound film production; first presentation of the Academy Awards, called the Oscars.

1928 Luis Buñuel and Salvador Dalí present a masterpiece of avant-garde film in France with *Un Chien Andalou (An Andalusian Dog)*; in Disney's *Steamboat Willy*, Mickey Mouse appears on screen for the first time.

1929 The American film industry accepts voluntary censorship of its movies through the Production Code, forerunner of today's ratings; it lays out a list of 11 "Don'ts" and 25 "Be Carefuls."

1930 Marlene Dietrich begins her international career with the film *The Blue Angel*. Together with

Brief Overview of the History of Film

Greta Garbo, Jean Harlow, Mae West and Zarah Leander, she introduced a new type of female star: the *femme fatale*. Simultaneously, the genre of the gangster film becomes popular.

1932 Films are accepted for the first time in the program of Venice's art biennial, now the Venice Film Festival.

1933–39 Musicals and dance films with stars like Fred Astaire and Ginger Rogers are among the most heavily attended films; the child star Shirley Temple (b. 1928) is the most successful star in the United States.

Around 1935 The British documentary film school sets new standards for the combination of aesthetics and realism.

1936 Chaplin's *Modern Times* is one of the last films to be released without a spoken word, and nevertheless becomes an enormous success.

1937 Disney presents the first feature-length cartoon film with *Snow White and the Seven Dwarfs*.

1939 Jean Renoir films his cinematic master-piece, *The Rules of the Game*; Selznick produces one of the first three-strip Technicolor films, *Gone with the Wind*, which can be viewed as the commercially most successful film of all time (accounting for inflation).

From 1940 Actresses like Ingrid Bergman, Lauren Bacall and Katharine Hepburn establish the new type of star with the confident "good bad girl," alongside the continuing existence of the *femme fatale*. Screwball comedy establishes itself as a new genre; the shadow-filled films of the *film noir* reflect the uncertainty brought about by the Second World War.

1941 *Citizen Kane* marks a high point in realistic film art.

1942 Michael Curtiz films *Casablanca*, a melodrama in the style of *film noir*, which later turns into a cult film of the new cinema-loving audience in the 1960s and 1970s.

1945 Roberto Rossellini presents the first neorealistic film with *Open City*.

1946 First film festival in Cannes.

1947 The rise of the new mass medium of television begins in the United States in the most commercially successful year ever for the American film industry.

1948 A Supreme Court judgment to break up the cartels ends the secret monopoly of the five large Hollywood studios and forces them to separate from their movie theater chains.

1950 The arrest of the Hollywood Ten, who had refused to testify during the first hearings of the Committee on Un-American Activities, introduces the period of McCarthyism, in which an anti-Communist witch hunt unfolds against personalities in public life.

1951 Akira Kurosawa is the first Japanese to receive an international film prize with the Golden Palm (Cannes) for *Rashomon* and directs worldwide interest to Asian cinematic art; in the United States, drive-in movie theaters rapidly become more popular and more plentiful. At their height they account for up to one quarter of all movie receipts.

1953 The first CinemaScope film, *The Robe*, premieres in New York.

1954 Introduction of television in the Federal Republic of Germany. In the United States, 65 percent of all households already have one television set, which leads to a great decline in movie attendance. The film industry combats the competition with the introduction of technical innovations like color film and wide screen film, stereo sound, and the less successful 3-D movies and aroma cinema.

1955 James Dean and Elvis Presley are the superstars of the screen. Their films demonstrate the intensified orientation of the film industry toward an increasingly youthful audience.

1956 Brigitte Bardot begins her film career and, along with Marilyn Monroe, embodies the new ultra-femine type of star, the naive sex-bomb.

1958 Truffaut's *400 Blows* begins the *Nouvelle Vague* (New Wave) in France.

1959 With his use of the technique in *Breathless*, Jean-Luc Godard elevates the film cut to a prominent artistic device.

1960 Alfred Hitchcock's thriller *Psycho* is only one example of the Master of Suspense's sublime manipulation of suspense and surprise; in Frankfurt am Main, the first Western European drive-in opens.

1962 The appearance of *Dr. No* featuring James Bond, agent 007, marks

Brief Overview of the History of Film

the start of the longest running film series to date.

1963 The flop of the largest monumental film to date, *Cleopatra*, almost brings Twentieth Century Fox to ruin.

1964 Sergio Leone begins the successful series of Italian-made "spaghetti westerns" with *A Fistful of Dollars*.

1967 Warner Brothers is the third studio to be sold to a large entertainment conglomerate (Seven Arts).

1968 Kubrick set new standards for the genre of the fantastic film with *2001: A Space Odyssey*.

1971 In Frankfurt, the first communal program theater opens despite the strong protests of commercial theater owners.

1974 Steven Spielberg's meteoric career begins with the sensational box office success of *Jaws*, one of the first films of the rejuvenated New Hollywood in which films' climaxes are more often comprised of chase scenes and violence than love scenes, and whose superstars are therefore seldom women, but men like Harrison Ford, Arnold Schwarzenegger and Robert de Niro.

1975 A new, worldwide market for home video recorders and video stores begins to develop.

1977 George Lucas' breathtaking science-fiction fairy tale *Star Wars* showcases the newest technical achievements of the special effects industry.

1978 R. W. Fassbinder, the most successful representative of the new

German film, achieves international recognition with *The Marriage of Maria Braun*. Woody Allen's *Annie Hall* receives four Oscars; the director, however does not accept the award out of protest against Hollywood.

1979 Volker Schlöndorff's filming of Günter Grass' novel *The Tin Drum* is the only German film to date to have received an Oscar in the category of Best Foreign Film; the first multiplex cinema in the world opens in Toronto, offering an infrastructure that integrates dining and shopping along with the highest technical standards for movie theaters, which turns the cinema into a new type of leisure experience.

1980 The elaborately staged fantasy fairy tale, *à la* Spielberg's *E.T.*, and action adventure films along the lines of the Rambo series starring Sylvester Stallone, establish themselves as the leading genres of the 1980s.

Mid-1980s Media behavior in the United States and Western Europe has changed fundamentally. Video recorders and home computers are found in almost every household; cable TV establishes itself.

1985 Germany's most successful female director, Doris Dörrie, succeeds with *Men*, a cinema hit which introduces the era of the new German film comedy.

1988 Robert Zemeckis demonstrates the advanced possibilities of digital composition in a

combination of animation and real film in *Who Framed Roger Rabbit?*

1990 The success of the movie *Pretty Woman*, whose open ending was changed into a fairy-tale happy ending after the strong protests of a test audience, demonstrates that the worldwide film audience continues to cling to the American dream of the rise of the underdog and a great, all-conquering love.

1991 With the success of *Terminator II*, Arnold Schwarzenegger establishes himself as one of the top paid Hollywood stars and becomes the model for screen heroes of the 1990s who, like his top competitor Sylvester Stallone, more and more frequently is also the producer of his films.

1992 The film premiere of the director's cut of Ridley Scott's *Blade Runner* shows how masterpieces can be mutilated even today by the invasiveness of the money man.

1993 Cinematic technique seems to know no boundaries since the computer-generated reincarnation of extremely realistic dinosaurs in Spielberg's *Jurassic Park*.

1994 Kevin Costner goes swimming with *Water World* and winds up with the most spectacular flop of the 1990s.

1995 The toy adventure *Toy Story* is the first entirely computer-animated movie.

1997 Filmed at a cost of 285 million dollars, James Cameron's *Titanic* is the most expensive movie of all time.

Bibliography

Bibliography

Allen, R., and Gomery, D. Film History: Theory and Practice. New York: Newbery Award Records, 1985.

Altman, Rick. The American Film Musical. London: British Film Inst., 1989.

Armes, Roy. A Critical History of the British Cinema. London: Secker & Warburg, 1978.

Baatz, Willfried. Photography: An Illustrated Historical Overview. Hauppauge, NY: Barron's Educational Series, 1997.

Balio, T., ed. The American Film Industry. Madison: University of Wisconsin Press, 1976.

Balio, T., ed. Hollywood in the Age of Television. Boston: Unwin Hyman, 1990.

Barnouw, E. Documentary: A History of Non-Fiction Film. Oxford: Oxford University Press, 1974.

Barton Palmer, R. Hollywood's Dark Cinema: The American Film Noir. New York: Twayne, 1994.

Barton Palmer, R., ed. Perspectives on Film Noir. New York: G.K. Hall, 1996.

Bering, Rüdiger. Musicals: An Illustrated Historical Overview. Hauppauge, NY: Barron's Educational Series, 1997.

Bogdanovich, Peter. Who the Devil Made It. New York: Knopf, 1997.

Bordwell, David. The Cinema of Eisenstein. Cambridge, MA: Harvard University Press, 1993.

Bordwell, David, J. Staiger, and K. Thompson. The Classical Hollywood Cinema. London: Routledge & Kegan Paul, 1985.

Braudy, Leo. The World in a Frame: What We See in Films. Chicago: University of Chicago Press, 1976.

Burrows, Elaine, ed. British Cinema Sourcebook. London: Brit. Film Inst., 1995.

Canemaker, J., ed. Storytelling in Animation. Los Angeles: Am. Film Inst., 1989.

Coe, Brian. The History of Movie Photography. Westfield, NJ: Eastview Ed., 1981.

Corner, J., ed. Documentary and the Mass Media. London: Edward Arnold, 1986.

Crisp, Colin. The Classic French Cinema, 1930–1960. Bloomington: Indiana University Press, 1997.

Elsaesser, T. New German Cinema: A History. Basingstoke, UK: Macmillan/British Film Inst., 1989.

Gomery, D. The Hollywood Studio System. London: Macmillan, 1986.

Grant, Barry Keith, II. Film Genre Reader II. Austin: University of Texas Press, 1995.

Hayward, Phillip, and Tana Wollen. Future Visions: New Technologies of the Screen. London: British Film Inst., 1993.

Hitchcock on Hitchcock: Selected Writings and Interviews, ed. by Sidney Gottlieb. Berkeley: University of California Press, 1995.

Hollis, R. and B. Sibley. The Disney Studio Story. New York: Crown, 1988.

Kaes, A. From "Hitler" to "Heimat:" The Return of History as Film. Cambridge, MA: Harvard University Press, 1989.

Kaplan, E. Ann. Women and Film: Both Sides of the Camera. London: Routledge, 1983.

Kent, N. Naked Hollywood. London: BBC Books, 1991.

Kerr, Walter. The Silent Clowns. London: Da Capo, 1990.

Kuenzli, Rudolph E., ed. Dada and Surrealist Film. Cambridge, MA: MIT Press, 1996.

Leyda, Jay. Kino: A History of Russian and Soviet Film, 3d ed. London: George Allen & Unwin, 1983.

Mast, Gerald, Marshall Cohen, and Leo Braudy, eds. Film Theory and Criticism, 4th ed. Oxford: Oxford University Press, 1992.

McCann, Richard Dyer, ed. The Silent Comedians. Lanham, MD: Scarecrow Press, 1993.

McFarland, Brian, ed. Sixty Voices: Celebrities Recall the Golden Age of British Cinema. London: British Film Inst., 1992.

Musser, Charles. Before the Nickelodeon: Edwin S. Porter and the Edison Manufacturing Company. Berkeley: University of California Press, 1991.

Nelmes, Jill, ed. An Introduction to Film Studies. London: Routledge, 1996.

Nowell-Smith, Geoffrey. The Oxford History of World Cinema. Oxford: Oxford University Press, 1996.

Nowell-Smith, Geoffrey, James Hay, and Gianni Volpi. The Companion to Italian Cinema. London: Cassell Academic, 1996.

Roy Levin, G. Documentary Explorations. New York: Doubleday, 1971.

Sarris, Andrew. The American Cinema: Directors and Directions, 1928–1968. New York: Dutton, 1968.

Schatz, Thomas. Hollywood Genres: Formulas, Filmmaking and the Studio System. New York: McGraw-Hill, 1981.

Solomon, C., ed. The Art of the Animated Image. Los Angeles: American Film Inst., 1987.

Taylor, Richard, and Ian Christie, eds. Inside the Film Factory: New Approaches to Russian and Soviet Cinema. London: Routledge, 1991.

Vincendeau, Ginette. The Companion to French Cinema. London: Cassell Academic, 1996.

Index of Film Titles

Index of Film Titles

Index of Film Titles

Index of Film Titles

Index of Film Titles

Index of Film Titles

Index of Film Titles ... Index of Names

Index of Names

Index of Names